IT'S BEHIND YOU!

IT'S BEHIND YOU!

THE STORY OF PANTO

YOU!

PETER LATHAN

NEW HOLLAND

First published in 2004 by
New Holland Publishers (UK) Ltd
London • Cape Town • Sydney • Auckland

www.newhollandpublishers.com

Garfield House
86–88 Edgware Road
London W2 2EA
United Kingdom

80 McKenzie Street
Cape Town 8001
South Africa

14 Aquatic Drive
Frenchs Forest, NSW 2086
Australia

218 Lake Road
Northcote
Auckland
New Zealand

ISBN 1 84330 736 7

Publishing Manager: Jo Hemmings
Senior Editor: Jane Morrow
Designer: Gülen Shevki
Production: Joan Woodroffe

Reproduction by Modern Age Repro Co., Hong Kong
Printed and bound in Malaysia by Times Offset (M) Sdn Bhd

Front cover: Nigel Ellacott and Peter Robbins as the Ugly Sisters; photo-
graph courtesy of *Essentials* magazine and photographer Steve Lyne
Inside front flap: Modern-day Clown; photograph by Peter Lathan
Spine: David Jason et al in *Cinderella*; photograph by Peter Lathan
Back cover: *Peter Pan* stage scene; photograph courtesy of
Qdos Entertainment
Inside back flap: Mark Seymour as Dame Trot and Steven Day as
Silly Billy in a 2002–3 production of *Jack and the Beanstalk*;
photograph courtesy of Nigel Ellacott
Page 1: Simon Bashford as Ugly Sister; photograph courtesy of
Simon Bashford and photographer W. A. Bennett
Page 2: Marc Seymour as Dame Trot in a 2002–3 production of
Jack and the Beanstalk; photograph courtesy of Nigel Ellacott
Page 5: Simon Bashford as Mother Goose; photograph
courtesy of Simon Bashford
Page 139: Peter Robbins and Nigel Ellacott as Ugly Sisters;
photograph by Alan Wood
Page 140: Keith Harris and Orville; photograph courtesy of
Qdos Entertainment

contents

3 THE MOST POPULAR PANTOS

INTRODUCTION

Is there anyone in Britain who's never been to a pantomime? Not many, that's for sure. It's a very British institution, more popular and certainly a lot older than the Derby or the FA Cup Final. Join me on a tour through the history of the only theatrical form we British ever invented!

'It's behind you!'
'Oh no, it isn't!'
'Oh yes, it is!'
'No, it isn't!'
'Yes, it is!'
'Isn't! Isn't! Isn't!'
'Is! Is! Is!'

And so it goes on! After all, it's panto and that's what panto is all about: joining in, shouting advice to the characters, booing the villain, cheering the hero. We've all done it – certainly as children and more than likely as adults, too. And of course we want to be in the Comic's gang and we'd be very happy for the Dame to throw some sweets at us. We take our kids because our parents took us, and in this way we're sharing something of our own childhood with them.

'A child who has never seen a pantomime,' said George Bernard Shaw in one of his letters in 1905, 'is a public danger.' Not everyone would agree, however. J. B. Priestley – possibly from intellectual snobbery or perhaps jealousy because his plays didn't attract the same size of audience – announced that he deplored 'the habit of Christmas playgoers flocking to the pantomime'. It's a tradition – a good old British Christmas tradition – with its origins lost in the mists of time, like so many of our traditions.

But what an odd tradition! A beautiful girl (played by a girl) and a handsome man (also played by a girl) fall in love with each other. They're helped by a young man (played by a man), who's in love with the girl but is willing to sacrifice his happiness for hers, and by a loud and brash woman (played by a man). An evil baddie tries to thwart the couple at every turn, but there is also a magical character who helps them. They're also helped by the people of the village (or town), who are all terribly good-looking and young and sing and dance a lot, and by the local children, who also do a fair bit of dancing.

Of course, everything turns out right in the end and the lovers marry and live happily ever after. And we knew the ending from the start! In fact, not only do we know the ending, we know the whole story. Pantomimes today are based on a limited number of stories which everyone knows. We're not there to find out what happens; we just want to know how they tell the story!

Odder still, when you think of it, is the fact that you'll find these shows everywhere, from the north of Scotland to westernmost Cornwall, and everywhere in between, in theatres big and small, performed by amateurs and professionals. (For many theatres, indeed, the panto is their lifeblood. It is what keeps them afloat financially for the rest of the year.)

Panto is a British phenomenon, an annual theatrical ritual. It is British, because wherever you find panto anywhere else in the world it's due to British influence; as Max Beerbohm said, it is the one art form invented in England.

But how on earth did the British, renowned the world over for their stiff upper lips and unemotional demeanour, come to invent a theatrical form which relies heavily on audience participation? And not just simple audience participation, in fact, but audience members shouting as loudly as they possibly can! Hysterical shouting, cross-dressing, sentimentality and magic? It's just not British! Foreigners look on in amazement, unbelieving. They don't understand. But then, who truly understands the traditions of other cultures? Indeed, who really understands their own? Well, it's always been like this. Our parents did it, as did their parents – and their grandparents. It's tradition!

But how did this tradition come about? What are its misty origins? It's a long story, but a fascinating one. Are you sitting comfortably?

Opposite: John Nettles as Captain Hook in *Peter Pan* at the Theatre Royal, Plymouth, in 2002.

WHERE IT ALL STARTED 1

WHAT HAVE THE ROMANS EVER DONE FOR US?

If we really stretch a point, we could say panto began with the Greeks. They certainly had a word for it; in fact, they invented the word 'pantomime' – παντομιμος – which translates as 'imitator of all'. But although it is the same word as the one we use, it means something quite different.

The Greek term for pantomime refers to what we now call a mime – someone like Marcel Marceau, who acts without speaking, whose exaggerated body movements mimic a whole range of emotions, ideas and things (literally an 'imitator of all'). In fact, if you mention the word 'pantomime' to anyone anywhere else in Europe today, that's the picture that will come to mind.

We have records of early Greek mimes stretching back to the fifth century BC. Fragments of the work of Epicharmus (c. 540–450 BC), the earliest known mime writer, survive, but all they show is that these mimes involved scenes from ordinary domestic life and, probably, farces based on mythology.

We do know a bit more about Roman mime. It usually had a satirical edge but its main preoccupation was with vice. Plots most often centred around adultery and usually featured naked women. In fact, there is evidence that actual sexual intercourse took place on-stage! It is also said that occasionally condemned criminals were executed in a scene which required a killing. The Roman Pantomimus, however, was a different thing altogether. Dressed like a tragic actor, the Pantomimus wore a mask and his performances were accompanied by music. Posture and gesture were the main tools of his trade and his was considered a refined art, often patronized by emperors and the imperial court.

The origins of what was to become, many centuries later, the British pantomime can be traced back to the Romans' *Fabulae Atellanae* (Atellan Stories), which were rather crude and earthy improvised farces, performed first in Campania, in southern Italy, where they took their name from the town of Atella. They used stock masked characters – the

Page 12: Dorothy Pointing and Fay Compton in *Dick Whittington*, in 1932.

Left: Marcel Marceau, the most famous modern mime, and an exponent of the kind of performance Europeans call pantomime.

simpleton, the gullible old fool, the glutton, the hunchback – and the plots were traditional and handed down orally from generation to generation until they became a literary form in the first century BC. Only a few fragments of the 'literary' *Fabulae* have survived, but they shared certain elements with the more sophisticated Roman Comedy, as exemplified by the plays of Plautus (251–184 BC) and Terence (190–150 BC).

Plautus is an interesting character. He is said to have spent his whole life in the theatre and to have written about 150 plays of which 21 have survived. We are not even sure if he was one man or two. His name is usually given as Titus Maccius Plautus, but one writer, a generation later, talks of Plautus and Titus Maccius as being two separate people. As he was an actor as well as a playwright, it is possible that one was his stage name: Maccius could be derived from Maccus, the clown of the *Fabulae*. Be that as it may, he has had a huge influence over the centuries. His plays were, to begin with, translations of the New Comedy of Greece (it is hard to escape the influence

Above: Frankie Howerd as Lurcio in *Up Pompeii!* (1970). We can trace Lurcio's character right back through pantomime and the *Commedia dell'Arte* to Roman comedy.

of the Greeks), but were obviously influenced by the *Fabulae*, and they gave us a host of stock characters who keep popping up in all sorts of times and places.

For example, take Plautus' *Miles Gloriosus*. The central character in this play is the Braggart Soldier, who is swaggering, arrogant and cowardly, and was the inspiration behind Il Capitano in the *Commedia dell'Arte*, Pistol and probably Falstaff in Shakespeare, and even Sergius in Shaw's *Arms and the Man* (1898). His play *Menaechmi* was the inspiration for *The Comedy of Errors*, and *Aulularia* resurfaced centuries later as Molière's *L'Avare* (1668). We also see his influence very strongly in *A Funny Thing Happened on the Way to the Forum*, which even uses his characters' names, and in Frankie Howerd's *Up Pompeii!*.

But what has this to do with pantomime? To discover that, we have to jump forward to sixteenth-century Italy.

AND SO THE YEARS PASSED

Little is known about what happened in Italian theatre during the Middle Ages, but what we do know is that somehow traditional rustic farce, such as the *Fabulae Atellanae* and the literary drama derived from Plautus and Terence, survived in some form or other, developing, in the sixteenth century, into the *Commedia Erudita* and the *Commedia dell'Arte*.

The *Commedia Erudita* (the 'Learned Comedy') was a very literary form, based both on Roman Comedy and later Italian writers such as Boccaccio (1313–75). (Boccaccio's greatest work, *The Decameron*, was very similar to Chaucer's *Canterbury Tales*, in that it was a collection of short stories told by a variety of characters. Although instead of being pilgrims, the storytellers are shut up in a country house while the plague rages in the surrounding countryside.) Sometimes performed in Latin, sometimes in very literary and formal Italian, the *Commedia Erudita* was not for the common man and was firmly aimed at the aristocracy. In fact, it was usually performed by the *dilettanti*, young aristocratic amateurs. However, it had nothing to do with what was to become the British panto.

The *Commedia dell'Arte* was a different matter. Here is a true ancestor of our pantomime – and a form which is still occasionally played today. Appealing to the taste of the general public and performed by professionals (its name means the 'Comedy of the Artistes'), it was a fusion of lots of different influences: clowning, acrobatics, dance, music, slapstick, satire, farce, love stories … much like pantomime, really. And like pantomime, it was full of stock characters – types rather than individuals. The characters wore a half-mask and their costumes, too, were standardized, so that the audience recognized who they were from their first appearance onstage, before they ever said a word.

There was Il Capitano, the Captain, a soldier who was full of himself. He claimed to be a great lover, a military genius and a fearsome fighter, but when it came to the crunch he proved to be a cowardly braggart. This character can be traced back to Plautus's *Miles Gloriosus*.

Then there was Il Dottore, the Doctor. Like Il Capitano, the image he projected was the opposite of the truth. A fat old man, he claimed to be learned and talked constantly, usually in a mixture of real and made-up Latin. (The word *dottore* in Italian means simply 'learned man'.) Sometimes he was portrayed as a lawyer, sometimes as an academic and even, on occasions, as a medical doctor. By the end of the play, however, he was always shown up to be a fake, a quack.

Old men didn't do very well in the Commedia as they were always the 'baddies'. Pantalone was a rich miser with lots of servants whom he treated badly, as he did his daughter (often he was portrayed as the father of a beautiful young girl, who may well be one of the Lovers). He was usually lascivious and a womanizer, although in some of the cruder *canovacci* (the name for Commedia plays) it was made obvious that, although he had the inclination, he didn't have the ability!

Oldies but baddies, that was the way of things in the Commedia. But to be honest, the young didn't fare much better. Take the Lovers, for instance. The hero and

Left: An etching of Il Capitano, the braggart soldier of the *Commedia dell'Arte*.

Above: Pantalone, the Commedia's rich old miser.

Right: Brighella, one of the Commedia's servants, the *Zanni*.

in bright colours. Their costumes weren't stock costumes either, but they wore whatever was fashionable at the time. They were exaggerated versions of the male and female ideals of the particular time and place.

Then there were the servants, the *Zanni*. The number of servants who appeared in the plays depended largely upon the number of actors available, but usually there were at least two. There was quite a number to choose from: the unreliable Brighella; the unscrupulous Scaramuccia (who became Scaramouche in the plays of the French comedy writer Molière); the naive Pedrolino (who became Pierrot in the French version of the Commedia and lasted until the last century in the end-of-the-pier Pierrot shows found in many seaside towns in the UK); Pulcinella, who later became Mr Punch; the amoral Arlecchino, who entered the British pantomime as Harlequin; and, of course, there was the female servant whom we still associate with Harlequin, Columbine (originally Columbina).

The *Zanni* provided the sub-plot and the physical humour. Like the servants in Plautus's plays, they delighted in subverting their masters, and so they would help the Lovers. Columbina, for example, was usually the heroine's maid.

These were the stock characters: characters whom the audience would recognize from their costumes and masks – even from their stance – and would know how they would behave. There were no surprises in the Commedia. The characters' names might change but they were still recognizably the same; the situation might change, but the plot didn't; the words would definitely change, but the way they were spoken wouldn't.

The similarities between the Commedia plays and modern pantomimes are clear. We know exactly what to expect from each character – how they dress, how they speak, the kind of thing they'll say – and we know that, no matter what obstacles are placed in the way of

heroine perhaps? Was their passion moving? Were they consumed by that passion? Not at all: they were in love with the idea of being in love – and with themselves. They drooped around the stage and sighed mightily. They were so busy declaring their love *for* each other *to* each other that they didn't actually get round to doing anything about it. Nonetheless their love lay at the centre of the action – as it does in modern pantomime.

Sometimes the girl, who might have been called Silvia or Isabella or any other 'romantic' name of the time, would be the daughter of Pantalone, who promised her in marriage to one of the other old men. Or else she might have been Pantalone's ward and he wanted to marry her himself, either because of his lust or to get his hands on her inheritance. But she, of course, was in love with our hero.

Alone of all the Commedia characters, the Lovers didn't wear masks: they wore make-up. Usually their complexions were white with the features drawn on the Principal Boy and Girl, love will conquer.

In the beginning, before the Commedia itself became a literary form, the companies moved from town to town, city to city, and performed in the open air. The performers would, we are told, make numerous references to the place they were performing and the people who were locally or even nationally famous. The dialogue was improvised, with the actors feeding off the audience's reactions. Each actor (and actress, for there was no ban on women appearing on the stage, as there was in England) specialized in a particular part (and parts could even be inherited from parents) and would have a store of speeches (and probably sight-gags, too), which they could produce more or less instantly. It's likely, too, that companies had set scenes

MADAME AURIOL AS COLUMBINE. 46.
London Published by J.REDINGTON, 73.Hoxton Street, Formerly called 208 Hoxton Old Town.

(and certainly had set visual gags) which they could incorporate into the performance.

You can imagine the discussions before a performance: 'I don't think we should do the fly-eating gag. It died the death last time we were here.'

'What about your mad doctor speech? That always goes down well.'

Not so very different from modern panto, where the comics will often get together and decide what gags they're going to work into the performance.

'Right, we'll do the "Will you lend me two quid?" gag in the first act.'

'Should we do the decorating or the ironing sketch?'

'I think Cinders and I should do the Y Dance gag.'

I suspect that many of our traditional panto gags and sketches may well date back to the Commedia.

Opposite top: Bill for Madame Auriol as Columbine, one of the Commedia characters who featured in pantomime right through to the second half of the nineteenth century.

Opposite bottom: 'In the wings during pantomime' – from *The Day's Doings*, 23 December 1871. Here we see the wide range of characters in the late nineteenth-century panto – far more than we ever see today.

We call them gags, but the Commedia name was *lazzi*, which translates as 'jokes'. In fact, many of the *lazzi* were quite extended, such as the Y Dance.

As performances were held out of doors and audiences were usually quite unsophisticated, performances were very physical and slapstick comedy was a major ingredient. In fact it is from the Commedia that we get the word 'slapstick'. The slapstick was Arlecchino's favourite weapon:

a paddle made from two pieces of wood which were joined together so that, when he hit someone (which he often did), it produced a loud slapping sound.

Clearly, there are significant elements of the Commedia in pantomime. But how did a popular and unwritten theatrical form from sixteenth-century Italy so strongly influence a British Christmas entertainment? Italian Commedia companies must have visited England at some stage. In fact, we know that they did, on at least two occasions: one appeared in 1577 and another performed before Queen Elizabeth I in 1602, so it does seem likely that others would have toured the country during the period. But if they did, they didn't really catch on and in fact it was the French, not the Italians, who brought the Commedia across the Channel.

☆ THE Y DANCE ☆

Buttons says to Cinderella, 'Cinders, do you know many modern dances?'

'Oh yes,' she replies.

'Do you know the Y Dance?'

'No, I don't think I've come across that one.'

'Would you like me to teach you it, Cinders?' Buttons asks.

'Oh yes please, Buttons,' she replies.

'Right then,' says Buttons. 'First we have to stand very, very close to each other.'

'Like this?' she asks, standing toe to toe with him.

'That's right. Now, you take your right hand', he takes it, 'and put it here.' He puts it on his left buttock.

'Is this right, Buttons?' Cinders asks.

'Oh yes,' says Buttons.

'And then?'

'And then,' says Buttons, 'you put your left hand – here.' And he places her left hand on his right buttock.

'Like this?' she asks again.

'Oh yes!'

'And then?'

'And then I put my right hand here.' And he places it on her left buttock.

'And then?'

'And then, I put my left hand here' – on her right buttock.

'And then?' she asks.

'And then,' he replies, 'why dance?'

This is a very old gag, used in many a panto over the years! I used it myself in a show my company, KG Productions, did for a community workers' conference – they thought it was hilarious! The age of a gag never stops an audience from laughing!

IT'S ALL THE FAULT OF THE FRENCH

Strange as it may seem, although the Commedia was probably *the* major influence on the development of the British pantomime, its influence was far from direct. In fact, when it made its appearance in the sixteenth and seventeenth centuries it had little effect at all. Even though the English didn't take to it that much, the very first English play in which Harlequin – who was to become the central character – appeared was written as early as 1607. This was *The Travailes of the Three English Brothers* by John Day.

It was the French who made the biggest impression with their version of the Commedia. In essence what they did is take over the Commedia, alter it and then bring it to England under the name 'Italian Night Scenes'. In this way the French directly influenced the only theatrical form that originated in England!

In the late seventeenth century a number of Italian Commedia companies appeared in France and made a big impression. The company of Tiberio Fiorilli actually settled in Paris at the Petit Bourbon theatre. So popular did it prove that in 1680 it received the royal seal of approval from Louis XIV, who gave it the title the *Comédie-Italienne* (to distinguish it from the *Comédie-Française*) and it moved into a new home at the Hôtel de Bourgogne. There it stayed until 1697, when the satire, which had always been part of the Commedia, proved too much and the Italian actors were expelled from France. It was reformed in 1716 and the process of becoming more French and less Italian, which had begun almost from its arrival in France, intensified and it moved into sentimental comedy with scripts written by French writers. In 1720, for instance, Marivaux

Above: Panel from a series of pictures painted by Andien de Clermont in 1742 showing *Commedia dell'Arte* scenes.

wrote two plays for the company, *L'Amour et la Verité* and *Arlequin Poli par l'Amour*. Later it transformed itself again and moved into *Opéra-Bouffe* (comic opera), merging in 1801 with the Théâtre Feydeau to form the *Opéra-Comique*, and no more was seen of the French version of the *Commedia dell'Arte*.

In 1673, before receiving the royal stamp of approval, Tiberio Fiorilli's company came to London, where it was a sensation. This led to the arrival of other French companies performing what they called *ballets-pantomimes*. These dance–mime performances became quite the rage in London, and theatre managements – then, as now, eager to put bums on seats – began to incorporate them into their own shows. They became afterpieces: short performances after the main event. These days, when a three-hour show is considered long, and when performing an uncut version of *Hamlet* is brave, it is hard to believe just how long audiences were willing to stay in the theatre a couple of centuries ago.

Those of a certain age, such as myself, will remember the cinema programmes of our youth: a number of trailers for forthcoming shows, one or

more shorts (possibly a documentary), Pathé or other news feature, a second feature and, finally, the main feature – the big picture. In the eighteenth century, and for much of the nineteenth century, theatre programmes had a similar format: a number of short performances of a variety of different kinds, then the main production, and finally an afterpiece.

So the *ballets-pantomimes* changed their name and became 'Italian Night Scenes'. As the name suggests, they consisted of dance and mime and were very much in the slapstick mode. The plots were very simple, usually involving some sort of disagreement between two of the (stock) characters, which led to the slapstick action. By 1715 they had

become a regular feature of the programme at the Lincoln's Inn Fields Theatre and proved so popular that other theatres started to follow suit.

Although called Italian Night Scenes, the settings were very English, such as an inn or a fair, and the central character was Harlequin. He was originally one of the Commedia's *Zanni*, but was now to become a regular on the English stage, and was the character who ushered in the new theatrical form of pantomime.

HARLEQUIN – THE MAIN MAN

Harlequin had a long pedigree, stretching from the *Fabulae Atellanae* through Plautus to the *Comédie-Italienne*. Arlecchino, one of the *Commedia dell'Arte*'s *Zanni*, was a servant; cowardly, superstitious, always broke and completely amoral. His clothes were those of a peasant and patched with large pieces of different coloured fabrics. His mask had small eyes, arched eyebrows and a wrinkled forehead. He carried a short wooden sword – possibly a remnant of the phallus of the Roman low comedy – which transformed into the slapstick.

By the early seventeenth century, Arlecchino had developed into a valet and had become a little more sophisticated, at least on the surface. In fact, he was rather gullible but clever. His amoral nature remained and he became very amorous, something which usually got him into trouble. Fortunately his cleverness was able to extricate him from the scrapes his amorousness got him into. In France, as 'Arlequin', he became elegant and very worldly-wise,

but retained his impudence, his cunning and his lasciviousness.

Although Harlequin – an anglicized version of his French name – found most favour in England as part of the afterpieces mentioned on pages 18–19, he did appear in some more mainstream plays. In 1677, just four years after Fiorilli's company performed in London, Harlequin appeared in *Scaramouche a Philosopher* by Edward Ravenscroft, which is possibly the first English play to use a Commedia plot. In 1685 an actor called William Mountfort wrote *The Life and Death of Dr Faustus*, which he described as 'a harlequinade in the Italian manner'. Then in 1687, England's first major female playwright, Aphra Behn, wrote *The Emperor of the Moon*, which was a farce-opera based on a Commedia plot.

By the time of the afterpieces, which became known as Harlequinades, his character had changed again. He gained mystical, even magical, powers. His slapstick became a *batte* (anglicized to 'bat') and was a kind of magic wand. One touch would set off a magical transformation: a cottage would change to a palace, a shop to a cave, or piles of junk into soldiers. Here we see the origin of the traditional transformation scene in *Cinderella*, in which her rags turn into a beautiful ball gown, a pumpkin into a coach and mice into horses. The man

Left: John Rich, also known as John Lun, acclaimed as the greatest Harlequin ever. Only semi-literate and with a poor speaking voice, he began playing Harlequin so that he wouldn't have to talk!

Opposite: A modern Harlequin in the traditional multicoloured costume, from a 1970s production.

☆ THE LINCOLN'S INN FIELDS THEATRE ☆

The Lincoln's Inn Fields Theatre, the birthplace of pantomime, started life as a tennis court: it was known as Lisle's Tennis Court. This, of course, was not lawn tennis as we know it today, but Real (i.e. Royal) Tennis, an indoor game with very different rules from those of the modern game.

In 1660 Sir William Davenant had the site converted to theatre use, installing the first proscenium arch stage in England and making it also the first professional theatre to have changeable scenery. The first production was his own play *The Siege of Rhodes* and he went on to present work by Shakespeare (Davenant was rumoured to be Shakespeare's illegitimate son), Dryden and other classic authors. He and his company moved to the Dorset Garden in November 1671 and, early the next year, when the Theatre Royal Bridges Street burned down, Thomas Killigrew moved in to the Lincoln's Inn Fields Theatre with his company.

In 1674 or 1675 it reverted to being a tennis court again and stayed that way for the next 20 years. In 1695 Thomas Betterton moved in with his company, which included the famous actress Anne Bracegirdle. However, ten years later it again fell into disuse until, in 1714, Christopher Rich took it over and began its restoration. He died the same year and the work was completed by his son, John.

The revamped theatre, seating 1,400 people, became the 'home of pantomime' until, with the money earned by the success of *The Beggar's Opera* in 1728, Rich built the new Covent Garden Theatre and moved there in 1732. During the subsequent 12 years or so Lincoln's Inn Fields was occasionally used but was demolished in 1748. The site it once occupied is now the Royal College of Surgeons.

responsible for this new Harlequin was John Rich (1681–1761), the manager of the Lincoln's Inn Fields Theatre. As we shall see, Rich, more than anyone else, has the right to be called the 'father of English pantomime'.

Rich, under his stage name, John Lun, played Harlequin for many years and gained the reputation of being arguably the greatest Harlequin ever. His first appearance was always spectacular. At various times he popped out of a lake, burst out of a furnace and was even hatched out of an egg! So expressive was his miming and so highly regarded his performances that it was felt that no one could compete and so, in 1759 at Drury Lane, in a Harlequinade produced by David Garrick, Henry Woodward actually spoke, mimicking the croaky voice which Arlequin had acquired in the *Comédie-Italienne*. So great was the Rich influence, however, that this innovation did not last and Harlequin remained silent.

In 1800, also at Drury Lane, the costume we now associate with Harlequin was first introduced. Instead of the patched peasant clothes, James Byrne created the now-traditional diamond-patterned, multi-coloured, spangled, body-fitting costume. He also invented what one feels tempted to call the 'cheat', which was a way of showing emotions without really having to act. Certain colours were made to represent emotions – yellow was jealousy, blue love, scarlet anger and mauve faithfulness – and Harlequin would pose and point his bat at a colour to show what he was supposed to be feeling. He even invented the convention that pointing at a black diamond meant he was invisible to the other characters on stage! This does seem to be cheating, but there was a reason for it because by this time Harlequin was declining in popularity, having been surpassed in the public's favour by the Clown (see page 31).

THE STAGE IS SET

It would be so much easier if there was a direct line of descent from the Commedia to pantomime and all we had to do was track the changes, but of course life is never that simple and there were other influences at work.

Let us begin with the masque, which was a popular form of entertainment in royal and aristocratic circles across Europe, particularly in Italy. At its most basic, a masque was the arrival at a gathering (a ball, perhaps, or a royal audience) of a group of masked people of the same sex, dressed in imaginative costumes, who would perform a brief dance and then join the company. Later the introductory dance became more complex and turned into a kind of dance drama, usually mythological or allegorical in subject matter, and then was followed by the company joining the revellers until called away by the presenter.

In England the masque developed further. Henry VIII and Elizabeth I loved them and they were the most popular entertainments at court. To the dance were added rich lyrical verses (paying compliments to the monarch, of course), beautiful costumes and elaborate scenery. The scenery was moved on- and off-stage often by complex machinery.

James I inherited the Tudors' love of the masque and two major artistic figures of the age were appointed to organize the increasingly elaborate events: Ben Jonson became court poet and Inigo Jones scenic designer, and between them they created some of the most elegant, spectacular and literary masques ever seen. Jonson also created the 'antimasque' (also called the 'antemasque', 'false masque' or 'antic masque'), which, like the satyr play that accompanied the Greek trilogy of tragedies, contrasted with the main event, being grotesque and comic.

As the masque declined, it left behind three things which were to have a major

influence on panto: the elaborate scenery and the stage machinery which moved it; the proscenium arch, which was invented to conceal the backstage workings from the audience, so making the whole piece even more impressive; and what we now call farce, which is what the antimasque became.

Meanwhile, in 1697, a book was published that was later to have a major effect on pantomime: Charles Perrault's *Mother Goose's Fairy Tales*. Containing, among others, the stories of *Puss in Boots*, *Cinderella*, *Sleeping Beauty* and *Little Red Riding Hood*, it became the source for the plots of some of the most enduring pantomimes.

Right: Ben Jonson, who became Britain's leading playwright after Shakespeare's death, was also James I's favourite writer of court masques.

It seems odd that legal matters could have an effect on the development of pantomime, but they did. Theatres had been closed by the Puritans under Cromwell during the Commonwealth (1649–59), and when they were reopened after the restoration of Charles II in 1660, only two were allowed to present spoken drama. In 1662 the King awarded 'Letters Patent' to Thomas Killigrew and William Davenant, allowing them to form acting companies. Killigrew formed The King's Servants at Drury Lane and Davenant The Duke of York's Servants at Lincoln's Inn Fields. However, Davenant didn't stay put and he and his company moved first to Dorset Garden and then, in 1732, to Covent Garden.

Inevitably, people began to regard the theatres as being licensed, and so for many years the only theatres allowed to present plays in London were Drury Lane and Covent Garden. In 1766 Samuel Foote was licensed to present plays at the Haymarket, but only during the summer months. After the Licensing Act (1737), Theatre Royals were set up in other towns and cities around the country. However, there were still only two legitimate theatres in London: Drury Lane and Covent Garden. To get around the law, other theatre owners had to present 'entertainments', music and dancing, alongside the spoken word. This clearly encouraged the growth of what was to become pantomime.

There's always been a puritan streak in the English. Where else would people believe that the moral thing to do is for men or boys to play women rather than let women appear onstage? There was a long history of actors being considered 'rogues and vagabonds', so you can imagine how they regarded actresses! It was not until after the Restoration (1660) that women were allowed to appear on the English stage, so we need look no further than this for the origin of the tradition of the Dame being played by a man. Although there is a more ancient precedent, the Morris Dancers' Betty (or Bessie), a very dame-like figure who is also to be found in the Mummers' Plays.

So now the scene is set for pantomime to burst onto the stage!

Below: A *bal masque* in the Galerie des Glaces, Château de Versailles, celebrating the marriage of the Dauphin Louis to Maria Theresa, Infanta of Spain, in February 1745.

☆ THE THEATRE ROYAL DRURY LANE ☆

Now the home of some of the biggest and most successful musicals, the Theatre Royal Drury Lane has been a major London theatre since the middle of the seventeenth century and was certainly a major influence on the development of pantomime.

Strangely enough, however, the first Theatre Royal was not in Drury Lane at all but in Bridges Street. It was built by Thomas Killigrew for The King's Servants in 1633. Unlike its successors, it was not a massive theatre, having a capacity of just 700, and it burned down in 1672.

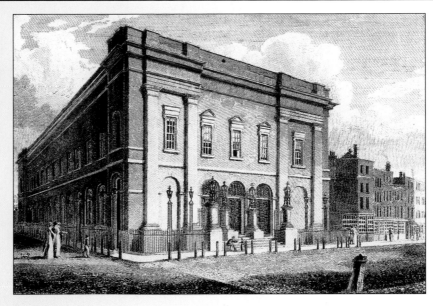

The first theatre to be built on the Drury Lane site opened in 1674 and is said to have been designed by Sir Christopher Wren. With a capacity of 2,000 it was considerably larger than its predecessor. Its foundations can still be seen under the stage of the current building. As a building, it was not highly regarded. John Dryden, whose plays were produced there, called it 'plain built – a bare convenience only'. The Drury Lane theatre's stage was in three sections: the front apron was the performance space, the middle had grooves in which the complex scenery moved, and the rear was for 'vistas' – the spectacular painted backdrops of distant scenes.

It wasn't the most popular theatre in London, partly because of its plainness and partly because it couldn't attract (or, at any rate, keep) top-class actors because of the universal dislike of Christopher Rich. It fared better once Rich left but struggled financially until it was managed by David Garrick from 1747 to 1776.

Garrick made a lot of changes, most of them in the way in which he worked with his actors. He stopped the practice of allowing members of the audience to sit on the stage, and his performance-related changes were very far-reaching. Rehearsals became serious; he insisted on a respectful and thoughtful approach to the classics; he brought to an end the practice of actors 'owning' a part. He also made major innovations in scenery, sound effects and lighting with de Loutherbourg, and he employed Robert Adam to redesign the interior in 1775.

The theatre was damaged in 1780 in the Gordon Riots, which led to a detachment of Guards being stationed there right through to 1896, although they failed to prevent an attempt on the life of George III in 1800. It was finally demolished in 1791 and rebuilt. The new theatre, which opened in 1794, was huge, with a seating capacity of 3,611. It didn't last long, however, for it too burned to the ground in 1809, in spite of having an iron safety curtain.

A new, slightly smaller theatre, seating 3,066, was opened in 1812 – the company having transferred to the Lyceum in the intervening years. Gas lighting was installed in 1817 and a portico in 1820, while a complete remodelling of the interior was carried out in 1822. In 1831, Nash's colonnade was added, having been removed from Regent Street. It's still standing today and is one of the the most popular venues in the West End.

CURTAIN UP!

The man raising the curtain, the director and star of the show, is John Rich (1681–1761), also known by his stage name of Lun (or Lunn). He was the son of Christopher Rich, who was part-owner and manager of the Drury Lane theatre and who was also largely responsible for the success of Italian Night Scenes – he was also reputed to be a bully, an extortionist and an all-round bad guy.

Complaints were made about Christopher Rich to the Lord Chamberlain, who took measures which effectively meant that he was sacked, although Rich only left when soldiers were sent into the theatre to remove him physically. He then took over the derelict theatre at Lincoln's Inn Fields and began to rebuild it. However, in 1714, he died before the rebuilding was completed and his son took over.

John Rich wanted to be an actor as well as run the theatre, but he was only semi-literate and his delivery was slow and boring, so he had little success until he had his great idea: pantomime. He took the term from the *ballets-pantomimes* of John Weaver, dancing master at the Drury Lane theatre, whose aim was to revive dance as a serious art form in England. He based his work on classical themes and ideas. Weaver's earliest known work was *The Cheats; or, the*

Tavern Bilkers, which was performed possibly as early as 1702, and was, as he put it, 'an attempt in imitation of the ancient Pantomimes'. It was not very successful. However, *The Loves of Mars and Venus* (1717), which was played as an afterpiece at Drury Lane and was the first performance in an English theatre to be called a pantomime, was much more successful.

The Loves of Mars and Venus certainly inspired John Rich (who had actually appeared in some of Weaver's productions), and in the same year he produced his first pantomime, *Harlequin Sorcerer*, in which he played Harlequin. This was the perfect role for him, because Harlequin does not speak (see page 22). Rich proved to be a talented mime and continued to play Harlequin until his death in 1761.

It was also in 1717 that Rich persuaded Weaver to join him at Lincoln's Inn Fields and they went on to produce many successful pantomimes, even though Weaver was none too keen on them, thinking them rather vulgar. Many innovations followed. In 1721 Rich incorporated references to contemporary events, in this case the South Sea Bubble scandal, in *The Magician; or, Harlequin a Director*, and in 1725, *Harlequin a Sorcerer, with the Loves of Pluto and Proserpine* included many spectacular effects, such as earthquakes, erupting volcanoes and fires.

In 1727 Rich had his biggest non-pantomime success, the first performance of John Gay's *The Beggar's Opera*, which ran for a record 62 performances and, as the saying went, 'made Gay rich and Rich gay'. More importantly, it gave him the money to open the Theatre Royal Covent Garden (now the Royal Opera House), which enabled him to put on

Left: David Garrick, leading actor and manager of the Theatre Royal Drury Lane, didn't like pantomime but had to put it on because of public demand.

Opposite: Pantalone and Columbine, from a modern Commedia production, *Joey and the Clown*.

☆ COLLEY CIBBER (1671–1757) ☆

Colley Cibber is best known today for his rewriting of Shakespeare's plays, particularly *Richard III*. He was a very influential figure in eighteenth-century theatre, beginning his career as an actor and working for a time with Christopher Rich. In 1710, along with Robert Wilks and Thomas Doggett, he took over Drury Lane, finally retiring from management in 1733, although he continued acting occasionally. He was a reasonably successful manager, although he did turn down *The Beggar's Opera*, which made John Rich a wealthy man.

Cibber was a playwright but also had geat success with adaptations, including Molière's *Tartuffe*. He also completed Vanbrugh's *A Journey to London*, two years after the latter's death in 1726, renaming it *The Provok'd Husband*. He became Poet Laureate in 1730.

He was not well liked and was considered to be a snob and full of conceit. So disliked was he by the poet Alexander Pope, for instance, that Cibber featured as King of the Dunces in Pope's mock epic *The Dunciad* in the edition of 1743.

Cibber staged the first pantomime at Drury Lane (*Queen Mab*) under pressure from David Garrick. He wasn't happy, and made a public apology for producing such a lowly form of theatre, but explained that it was pantomime or starvation for the actors! In his two-volume work *Apology*, he calls pantomimes 'the gin-shops of the stage'.

more spectacular productions than were possible at Lincoln's Inn Fields. He had a large following of fans, including George II, and his reputation for mime grew to almost mythic proportions.

Rich's pantomimes were so successful that others were forced to follow suit. David Garrick, who felt that pantomime would undermine serious theatre, staged his first pantomime, *Queen Mab*, at Drury Lane in 1750. Thereafter the two theatres were engaged in what can only be described as a war, each striving to outdo the other.

In 1753, for example, Garrick had a real waterfall onstage and in 1759 his *Harlequin's Invasion* introduced the very first hit song to come out of a pantomime, 'Hearts of Oak':

Come cheer up, me lads, 'tis to glory we steer
To add something more to this wonderful year.
To honour we call you, not press you like slaves,
For who are so free as the sons of the waves?
Hearts of oak are our ships
Jolly Tars are our men.
We always are ready –
Steady, boys, steady!
We'll fight and we'll conquer again and again!

But still it was Rich who set the pace, for his mime skills were legendary. His most famous performance was undoubtedly *Harlequin Hatched from an Egg by the Sun* (1741), which was often imitated but never equalled. This contemporary account shows why he was so highly regarded:

I saw him enact the hatching of Harlequin by the heat of the sun. This certainly was a masterpiece in dumb show; from the first chipping of the egg, his receiving of motion, his feeling of the ground, his standing upright, to the quick Harlequin trip around the empty shell, through the whole progression, every limb had its tongue and every motion a voice, which spoke with most miraculous organ to the understanding and sensation of observers.

(John Jackson, *History of the Scottish Stage*)

Although to his contemporaries it was Rich's performances for which he was best known, today he is recognized primarily as the man who set the pattern for pantomime that would last for almost two centuries and even influence its shape today. Among all his innovations, the most influential was the Harlequinade.

THE HARLEQUINADE

Rich's pantomimes were in two parts: a mythological or folk story; and the Harlequinade, which told in mime the comic adventures of Harlequin as he and his lover, Columbine, were pursued by her father, Pantaloon, and his servant, Pedrolino (Pierrot). Chase scenes were an essential part of the Harlequinade, as were the magic tricks done by Harlequin to get rid of the pursuers.

The actor playing Harlequin needed to be a mime, dancer and acrobat, for the Harlequinade was not spoken and the chase scene grew to involve jumping in and out of trap doors, through windows, or from great heights. As time passed, the acrobatics became more and more spectacular and dangerous to the performer. These scenes were interspersed with dances (usually romantic and featuring Harlequin and Columbine), songs and other interludes.

At first – and for a long time – the two parts of the play, the mythological and the Harlequinade, ran concurrently. This often meant that the audience quite literally 'lost the plot' as the action shifted from one part to the other, and then back again. But this disconnection between the two parts had to go and eventually the two were separated out. The mythological story became the Opening and, like the Italian Night Scenes out of which it grew, the Harlequinade ended the evening's entertainment and had little or no connection to the first part. It was not uncommon for members of the audience to arrive late for the performance, missing most or all of the Opening but in time for the Harlequinade. In fact, at one time certain theatres would return part of the entrance money to those who had to leave before the Harlequinade started.

The first pantomime to link the two parts together came after Rich's death, in 1761. This was *Robinson Crusoe; or, Harlequin Man Friday* and was staged at Drury Lane in 1781. It was attributed to Richard Brinsley Sheridan, author of *The Rivals* and *The School for Scandal*, who had taken over Garrick's share of the theatre in 1776 (although it has also

Above: The transformation scene from *Cinderella*, where her rags turn into a glamorous ballgown, a pumpkin into a coach, and mice into horses (Theatre Royal, Newcastle, c. 1970).

been attributed to his wife and other members of his family). This was a pantomime full of innovation, for Sheridan actually used Harlequinade characters in the Opening: Pantaloon torments Man Friday who, later, along with Crusoe, rescues both him and Pierrot from cannibals. It was, incidentally, a very successful panto, running for 38 nights, which was a long time in the eighteenth century.

After Robinson Crusoe, it became customary for the two parts to be linked by the device of revealing that the hero was, in fact, Harlequin, and the heroine Columbine. This happened at a point in the opening plot when it looked as though things were going very wrong for our hero and heroine. The revelation was brought about by transformation scenes, the remnants of which we still see today in *Cinderella*.

They began quite simply: outer costumes would be stripped away, sometimes by the use of strings or cords which flew them across the stage or down hidden trap doors – in the nineteenth century these scenes became increasingly complex and spectacular (see page 35). After the transformation scene, the knockabout comedy started and the plot of the opening section was more or less forgotten until the ending restored happiness to all who deserved it. Of course, Harlequin and Columbine lived happily ever after, or, at least, until the next pantomime.

Above: A chase scene from the children's book *The Christmas Pantomime*, c. 1890. The Chase scene was an essential part of every Harlequinade.

JOEY!

There are some performers in the history of English pantomime who stand head and shoulders above the others, not simply because of what they did onstage but because of their influence. John Rich was one, but another performer was to replace Rich's legacy with his own: Joseph Grimaldi (1778–1837).

Grimaldi began his stage career early at two years and four months of age. It nearly ended at the age of three when, playing a monkey at Sadler's Wells, he was being swung around by his father on the end of a chain. The chain broke and he was hurled into the stalls where, fortunately, he was caught by a member of the audience. Throughout his childhood he played a range of small parts and it was in 1800, at the age of 22, that he first played the part that was to make him a theatrical legend – the Clown.

The Clown had been a part of the English tradition of theatre since the Middle Ages. His theatrical origin is the Vice of the Morality Plays. These plays told a moral tale and, to make sure the message got home, the characters had names which showed their character, for example, Mercy, Justice, Temperance and Truth. Bunyan's *Pilgrim's Progress* (1672) is the well-known work which comes nearest to the Moralities, although it is in novel rather than dramatic form. The most well known of the Moralities to survive is *Everyman*. Some commentators regard Shakespeare's *Richard III* as a sophisticated version of the medieval Vice, but, in general, the Vice tended to become a comic character, being tricky and clever enough even to fool the Devil.

The Clown – same name, different origin – had always been a part of the Harlequinade. He was one of the *Zanni* (Servants) of the Commedia. However, he wasn't very important – essentially a buffoon, a stupid servant, he was the 'village idiot' of the Commedia and,

subsequently, of the Harlequinade. His earliest appearance in England was in Weaver's *Perseus and Andromeda* in 1725, and he remained very much a minor character until Grimaldi took over the part in *Peter Wilkins; or, Harlequin in the Flying World* at Sadler's Wells in 1800.

Grimaldi was to play Clown for the rest of his working life, constantly refining and redefining the role, and having an immense effect on the

MR GRIMALDI, as Clown.

Right: Joseph Grimaldi, whose playing of the Clown was so influential that even today clowns are known in the business as 'Joeys'.

Grimaldi's innovations were many. Apart from the costume and make-up, he changed the Clown's character, making him a mischievous (but loveable) rogue. He took over from Harlequin the role of the acrobat but added wit and subtlety, and not a little satire. He invented many of the gags which we still see in panto today: the string of sausages (also seen in Punch and Judy shows), and the butter on the doorstep were both originally devised and performed by Grimaldi. He was also a master of what have been called 'tricks of construction', assembling a motley crowd of various objects into something entirely different. In addition, he was the first to have what we could well call hit songs, such as 'Tippety Witchet' (1810) and 'Hot Codlins' (1819), which became so popular that, long after Grimaldi had retired, audiences demanded that the Clown sing them. Also, Grimaldi was the first to make extensive use of the catchphrase. In the transformation scene when he was revealed as Clown, Grimaldi would shout out, 'Here we are again!'

So inventive and entertaining were Grimaldi's performances, and so pervasive his influence, that Harlequin was knocked off the top spot in the Harlequinade and ended up playing second fiddle to the Clown. In fact, he was so good that no one could ever replace him. After his retirement, the Harlequinade began to fall from favour, and the Opening gradually assumed far greater importance.

performances of those who followed him. He began as he meant to go on: in *Peter Wilkins* he changed the costume, moving away from the servant's garb, and, most significantly of all, devising the white face make-up with the bright red cheeks which we still associate with clowns today.

In 1806 he moved to Covent Garden, where he had huge success in *Harlequin Mother Goose; or, The Golden Egg*. This established him as the leading pantomime performer of his day, and he was to play Clown either at the Wells or Covent Garden theatres for another 17 years, until, in 1824, at the age of 45, he was forced to retire, being virtually crippled by the number of major injuries he had sustained onstage during his career. He did make two farewell appearances in 1828: in his final one at Drury Lane he was actually carried on to the stage in a chair and did his performance seated.

Grimaldi's influence is still felt today, the Clown lives on in the comedians of the modern panto. We can draw, I would suggest, a direct line from Grimaldi (and hence from the Harlequinade, the Italian Night Scenes and the Commedia) through to Buttons in the modern *Cinderella*. But perhaps the greatest compliment to the master Clown of the nineteenth century is the fact that, even today, the Clown is still known as the 'Joey'.

Above: Charles Robinson as the pantomime Clown in *The Child's Christmas* by Evelyn Sharp.

Opposite: Grimaldi, the 'Michelangelo of Buffoonery', in *Harlequin and Mother Bunch, or The Yellow Dwarf*.

☆ THE GRIMALDI FAMILY ☆

The great Clown of the English pantomime, Joseph Grimaldi, was born into a theatrical family. His father was Giuseppe Grimaldi (c. 1710–88), an Italian dancer who worked in both Italy and France before coming to England in 1759, when he joined the company at Covent Garden, and his mother was a chorus girl called Rebecca Brooker, one of Giuseppe's mistresses (he was known for his philandering). When Joseph was born in 1778, his father was well over 60.

Giuseppe was himself the son of a dancer, who was nicknamed 'Iron Legs', and he was determined that his son should follow in his footsteps, making sure that he appeared onstage as soon as he could walk. Giuseppe was nicknamed 'Old Grim' and he lived up to that name. He beat young Joseph regularly – it is said that he even did so onstage – and his dissolute lifestyle, including his many mistresses, did not make for a happy family life. Rebecca and Joseph were left almost destitute after his death. Giuseppe played Harlequin at Drury Lane and was ballet master there under Garrick. Amazingly he swapped parts at the age of 71 to play Clown.

Joseph avoided the excesses of his father but his life was far from smooth. He was plagued by injuries caused by his acrobatic performances and he died in 1837 at the age of 59. His work was not, of course, confined to pantomime. He had great success in straight theatre, especially as Bob Acres in Sheridan's *The Rivals*.

Joseph Grimaldi married twice, his first wife dying after a year of marriage. His second wife, Mary Bristow, an actress, produced a son, Joseph Samuel William, born in 1802. Young Joseph also took to the stage and made his first appearance at the age of 13 in *Harlequin and Fortunato* at Sadler's Wells. He played Clowny-Chip, a sort of 'chip off the old block', along-side his father who, of course, played Clown. Young Joseph was well received by audiences and was his father's natural successor.

Immediately after the elder Joseph retired, the younger played Clown in *Harlequin and Poor Robin, or the House that Jack Built* at Covent Garden. This was a great success, but it was his last. He had inherited his grandfather's temperament and, as we say nowadays, went off the rails. He began drinking heavily, was in trouble with the law and not only did he have nothing further to do with his family, he was also dropped by the theatres. Eventually, just before his thirtieth birthday, he died an alcoholic, insane and in poverty.

THE GLORY YEARS

If the seventeenth century provided the fertile soil for the growth of pantomime, and the eighteenth helped it germinate, then it was in the nineteenth that allowed it to bloom. First there was Grimaldi, then spectacle took over. Next, the Harlequinade was reduced in importance and the Opening became the central feature. The story began to be more important than the knockabout comedy, and the story needed scenery – always an important part of the pantomime and the masque.

Already at the beginning of the nineteenth century another theatrical form, the Extravaganza, had been developed. It was characterized by a good deal of spectacular scenery and lavish costumes, and also featured music, rhyming couplets and light satire. By the 1830s these Extravaganzas were doing good business at the Lyceum and Olympic theatres, even taking business away from the pantomimes. In 1839, Madame Vestris (an actress and singer who, in 1830, became London's first ever female theatre manager) and J. R. Planché (the writer of the

Olympic's most successful Extravaganzas) took over Covent Garden and it was not long before the Extravaganza was absorbed within the Opening,

Below: *Dick Whittington* at the Theatre Royal, Exeter, in 1953. Waterfalls and other spectacular effects were common in pantos up until the 1960s, when they became too expensive to stage.

Opposite: Late nineteenth-century engraving showing the Star Trap ('trap' being short for trapdoor), the means by which the Clown made his unexpected appearance.

☆ THEATRE ROYAL COVENT GARDEN ☆

Covent Garden is so called because it used to be part of the garden of a convent. Like Drury Lane and Lincoln's Inn Fields, Covent Garden had enormous influence on the development of panto-mime. The first theatre to be built there was commissioned by John Rich and opened in 1732 with a performance of Congreve's *The Way of the World*. Its capacity was almost 3,000 and was enlarged in 1792. However, in 1808 it was destroyed by fire. A new theatre, based on the design of the Temple of Minerva on the Acropolis, opened the following year. It too had a capacity of 3,000. Gas lighting was installed in the entrance hall and the grand staircase in 1815, and two years later in the auditorium and on the stage.

However, it was dogged by financial problems and actually closed for five years between 1842 and 1847. After some refurbishment, it reopened in 1847 as the Royal Italian Opera House, boast-ing an increased capacity of 4,000. It fell victim to fire again and was burned to the ground in 1856. A new, smaller (2,141 capacity) theatre was built on the site and opened in 1858. From that time on, it specialized in opera, being renamed the Royal Opera House in 1939. In recent years the venue has been totally refurbished with the assistance of grants from the National Lottery.

leaving the Harlequinade as an increasingly unimportant little tailpiece.

At the same time, the diorama was developed. This was a long backcloth – often more than five or six times the width of the stage – on which was painted a continuous landscape. At each side of the stage there would be a large vertical roller and the cloth would be rolled from one to the other so that the scene would gradually change. (Film buffs or fans of Fred Astaire or Judy Garland will remember a diorama rolling back and forth during the song 'We're a Couple of Swells' in *Easter Parade*.) The artistry of the dioramas became increasingly complex as time went by, from simple panoramic landscapes, to seascapes (in *Harlequin and Friar Bacon; or, The Brazen Head* at Covent Garden in 1820 the diorama depicted the crossing of the Irish Sea), to events such as the royal progress of George IV through Scotland. In 1823 Drury Lane paid £1,380 for its diorama – a fantastic sum in those days and more than some theatres spent on the entire panto. In 1831 the same theatre paid for its scenery designer, Clarkson Stanfield, to go to Venice to ensure a realistic diorama for *Harlequin and Little Thumb*.

Then there were the aerial dioramas, which worked in exactly the same way except that they went up and/or down to simulate flight. An aerial diorama was first used in 1823 in *Harlequin and Poor Robin* at Covent Garden in which Clown and Pantaloon were carried from London to Paris in a hot-air balloon. Aerial dioramas are still seen occasionally in panto, especially in *Jack and the Beanstalk* when Jack climbs up to Giant Blunderbore's castle.

But these weren't the first spectacular effects. As early as 1804, Sadler's Wells rebuilt the stage so that it could be flooded and did so many times in the years that followed. In 1829 Covent Garden installed a huge water tank so that it could have a real waterfall onstage for *Jack in the Box*. Although they are not so common today, because of expense, I do remember such spectacular features in pantomimes in the 1950s, although the effects were hired in rather than being permanent installations. (The taste for spectacular scenery and effects continues to this day – for example the helicopter in *Miss Saigon* and the flying car in *Chitty Chitty Bang Bang*, which reputedly cost £750,000!) However, it was in the transformation scenes that there was the greatest competition between theatres and, probably, the most innovation.

Originally, transformation scenes signalled the end of the Opening and the start of the Harlequinade, with the characters of the Opening being transformed into Harlequin, Columbine, Pantaloon and the rest. As the Harlequinade declined after Grimaldi's retirement, the emphasis switched to the scenery, and designers used more and more complex stage machinery to create their transformations. One of the best known – and the most influential, because it sparked off many imitations – was in Planché's *Island of Jewels* at the Lyceum in 1849. Designed by the man who was to become one of the great set designers of the century, William Beverley, this featured the leaves of a palm tree gradually falling to reveal six fairies holding up an array of glittering jewels.

Following *Island of Jewels*, designers vied with each other to produce ever more impressive transformations, some lasting as long as 20 minutes. Scenery that slowly folded itself up or fell to the side, scenery that rose and fell at the same time (the top half being flown up to the roof while the bottom slid down rails to drop below the stage, revealing yet another set behind), gauzes that were opaque when lit from the front but transparent when lit from behind – every possible design was exploited in the struggle to produce the most spectacular transformation scene.

Lighting became increasingly important as the nineteenth century passed but, even in the previous century, stage lighting – usually candlelight – achieved an amazing degree of sophistication. Philippe Jacques de Loutherbourg at Drury Lane, for example, placed dyed silk in front of lamps, thus anticipating the gels which are part of the lighting designer's arsenal today. He even anticipated effects projectors by moving a silk screen painted with a cloud panorama in front of a bank of candles.

It was the arrival of gas lighting in the early nineteenth century, however, that gave the designer so much more scope. The first gas lighting was seen at the Lyceum in 1817. It had the advantage that it could be dimmed when required and so different intensities of light could be used across a set, a technique that set designers such as Beverley made full use of.

Then came limelight. Heating a piece of lime produces a much more intense light than gas, and producers were quick to make use of this new technology. However, set and costume designers had to be very careful, for the light has a greenish tinge which caused problems with certain colours. The first to use it was Macready at Covent Garden in 1826 in a pantomime called *Peeping Tom of Coventry*. Today we still speak of people being 'in the limelight' and old-fashioned theatre folk like myself still refer to follow-spots as 'limes'.

The Victorians were great ones for technology and delighted in the latest developments in machinery, so it is not surprising that they made such extensive use of it in theatre, but this emphasis was not their only contribution to the development of pantomime, as we shall see next.

WORDS, WORDS, WORDS

'What is't you read, my Lord?' Polonius asked.
'Words, words, words,' replied Hamlet.

Had Shakespeare been a creator of pantomimes, then 'words, words, words' would not have been his stock-in-trade, at least until the nineteenth century. Of course, the Licensing Act of 1737 made it illegal for any but the patent theatres to present spoken drama. Covent Garden and Drury Lane were the patent theatres and the leading exponents of pantomime, so there should have been no problem, but, as we have seen, John Rich was not a good speaker so he latched on to the non-speaking Harlequin as his speciality, which set the tone for all pantos that followed.

Garrick did try a speaking Harlequin in 1759, but it wasn't much of a success, and so for many years pantomimes at the two patent theatres (and at the Haymarket, which was allowed a patent for the summer months) were silent out of choice. Those at other theatres, both in and outside of London, were silent by necessity. But when the Harlequinade began to lose its importance and the Opening became the central feature of the pantomime, the spoken word became essential.

Fortunately, in 1843 – pretty good timing! – the Licensing Act was repealed and replaced by the Theatre Regulation Act, which allowed all theatres to present all types of entertainment. A good thing, certainly, but the Act also introduced something that was to bedevil British theatre right through to the 1960s – censorship. From 1851, all plays had to be submitted to and approved by the Lord Chamberlain's office (there was actually an 'Examiner of Plays') before they could be performed.

Edward Blanchard (1820–89) was the greatest writer of pantomimes of the nineteenth century. The son of a comedian, he wrote pantos for 40 years and for 37 of them was the writer of all the pantomimes

Above: E. L. Blanchard, the leading pantomime writer for 40 years, who collaborated on at least 100 in that time.

at Drury Lane. His first, in 1852, was *Harlequin Hudibras; or, Old Dame Durden and the Droll Days of the Merry Monarch*, and his last *Babes in the Wood*. Blanchard was known as the king of pantomime writers and wrote or collaborated on over 100 of them. Between 1856 and 1880, there were at least two of his pantos presented every year, and in 1874 there were four!

'The Prince of Openings' – or, as he was also known, 'The Hero of a Hundred Pantomimes', he actually didn't like the term pantomime and gave his pieces the name 'annuals', but history has made his dislike irrelevant!

Blanchard was a strange mixture of traditionalist and innovator. As an innovator he changed the Opening beyond recognition. His Openings were not simply written in rhyming couplets, which became the norm in the nineteenth century, but they were truly poetic. They were literary, with a strong moral tone and in many ways they were educational (something which was to become, inevitably, a Victorian tradition).

As a traditionalist, however, he desperately tried to save the Harlequinade, which was going into terminal decline after the retirement of Grimaldi. Blanchard even tried doubling – and once even tripling – the number of characters to keep it alive. But he eventually realized that the tradition, which stretched back to medieval Italy (or even earlier), was finished and so his 1883 production of *Cinderella* at Drury Lane was the first at that theatre to be performed without the Harlequinade.

He was also very much set against the idea of using Music Hall stars in panto. He felt – probably correctly – that they took liberties with his scripts and that the story got lost. However, the hard-headed manager, Augustus Harris, who referred to

☆ NELSON LEE ☆

Prolific as Blanchard was, his output didn't approach that of his rival, Nelson Lee (1806–72), who wrote around 200 pantomimes for a variety of theatres both in and out of London. His pieces had the same elevated and moral tone as Blanchard's but lacked the literary style of the younger man.

The son of a naval officer, Lee began his career in theatre as a juggler working as part of a touring company, Richardson's Travelling Theatre (for whom he wrote a number of pantomimes). He also worked at about half a dozen of London's theatres, including Sadler's Wells and the Adelphi.

Lee's most interesting pantomime was *Romeo and Juliet, or Harlequin Queen Mab and the World of Dreams*, in which he parodied Shakespeare's masterpiece.

Blanchard as 'the old man of the sea', would not be swayed. So Blanchard discovered, as has many a writer both before and after him, that if you want to work, you do what the one who holds the purse strings tells you to do!

Prolific though he was, Blanchard did not always write alone. He had a successful collaboration with Thomas Greenwood (1806–79), who was resident writer and, from 1843, joint-manager of Sadler's Wells. Greenwood retired from the managership in 1853 but continued writing until his death. Blanchard and Greenwood collaborated under the name 'The

Brothers Grinn', which was an example of another typical feature of Blanchard's writing – puns.

Puns are an important part of modern pantos, but the great days for panto-punning were the years of the mid-nineteenth century, and the acknowledged master was H. J. Byron (1834–84). Before moving on to Byron, however, we need to make a slight diversion and jump back to the seventeenth century.

Below: Illustration by Paul Renouard showing children who work in the pantomimes at Drury Lane receiving their lessons at the theatre's school (1889).

BURLESQUE

'Asleep, my love?

What? Dead, my dove?

Oh Pyramus, arise!

Speak! Speak!

Quite dumb.

Dead! Dead!

A tomb

Must cover these sweet eyes.'

Even today, audiences find Pyramus and Thisbe, the play-within-the-play in *A Midsummer Night's Dream*, hilariously funny. And quite right, too, for the overblown language it parodies is not restricted to bad plays of Shakespeare's time but can still be found in the more lurid novels of today. This delightful send-up is an early example of what was to develop into a full-blown genre of its own in the late seventeenth century. We call it parody – then it was known as burlesque. Unlike Shakespeare's play-within-the-play, burlesques were full-length productions, the purpose of which was to send up a style or even a genre of theatre. They weren't restricted to England – burlesque could be called an international movement, which culminated in Europe with work as diverse as that of Gilbert and Sullivan, and Offenbach. However, burlesque took a different direction in the United States, eventually becoming little more than a (rather tame) strip show.

In 1855, at the Adelphi Theatre, Mark Lemon, the first editor of *Punch*, attempted to unite the traditions of burlesque and pantomime in *Jack and the Beanstalk; or, Harlequin and Mother Goose at Home Again*, in which he introduced a new character, Burlesque himself. Generally, however, the influence of burlesque on pantomime was more indirect, coming by way of the Extravaganza, which had more or less absorbed burlesque by the middle

Left: Douglas Mounce as Widow Twankey in a 2001 production of *Aladdin* at the Queens Theatre in Barnstaple. Oversized bras are an essential part of every Dame's costume!

☆ MADAME VESTRIS ☆

Few women can be said to have had a major influence on the history of pantomime, but Lucy Elizabeth Bartolozzi (1797–1856) is one. Under her stage name, Madame Vestris, she became one of the most important figures in theatre in the first half of the nineteenth century, as an actress and singer, but, most important of all, as a theatre manager.

She made her first appearance onstage at Drury Lane in 1817 and went on to be one of that theatre's most popular actresses, as well as gaining similar favour at Covent Garden. She was highly regarded as an actress and singer, but her popular fame came from her widely admired legs! Because of her legs, she was in great demand for 'breeches parts', even playing characters such as Macheath in *The Beggar's Opera* at the Haymarket (see page 80 for more on the Principal Boy).

Madame Vestris was the first woman ever to manage a London theatre when, in 1830, she took over the Olympic Theatre in the Strand. Built in 1806, it was renamed the Little Drury Lane Theatre in 1813 and fell foul of the authorities and lost its licence. It was burned to the ground in 1849, rebuilt and then finally demolished in 1904.

Vestris's great claim to historical fame is her association with Planché and his Extravaganzas. They began working together almost as soon as she took over the Olympic, and they very quickly gained a reputation for lavish productions. Along with her second husband, actor Charles Matthews, Vestris took over Covent Garden in 1839 and repeated her success there, producing more and more amazing productions, until the couple ended up in prison for debt. In 1847, having served their sentences, the couple took over the Lyceum, which they ran with equal success – and equal financial trouble, for Vestris served another prison sentence for debt in this period – until 1855.

She made her final stage appearance in 1854 at the age of 57, although by then her health was failing. She died two years later, the first and – in spite of the financial vicissitudes – probably most successful female theatre manager in London.

---

of the nineteenth century. At the forefront of this new development – and here we return to where we left off on page 39 – was H. J. Byron.

Byron, unusually for someone who became an actor, playwright and theatre manager, did not come from a theatrical family. In fact, he began life as a medical student and then studied the law, but gave both up to work in theatre. He wrote a wide range of plays – straight plays (usually sentimental comedies), Extravaganzas, Openings, pantomimes – but was most famous in his day for his burlesques. Like the Extravaganzas, from which they became indistinguishable, the burlesques gradually merged into something that is rather more like our modern pantomime than the Opening/Harlequinade combination. Byron introduced Widow Twankey in *Aladdin and his*

Wonderful Lamp; or, the Genie of the Ring in 1856, and four years later gave us Buttons in *Cinderella; or, The Lover, the Lackey, and the Little Glass Slipper*. This burlesque was also the first to really develop the characters of the Ugly Sisters into something near to what we know today.

The emergence of what we might call the modern pantomime can be traced, very approximately, to the 30-year period between 1850 and 1880, when the Harlequinade vanished from all but the work of the most diehard of traditionalists. From then on, we see panto as *we* know it developing and growing into the big money-spinner for theatres both professional and amateur right across Britain.

Overleaf: Ian Adams and Jack Wild steal the show as the Ugly Sisters in *Cinderella*, in 1999.

LET'S ALL GO TO THE MUSIC HALL

'Let's all go to the Music Hall,
Where the stars are shining twice a night.'

Recently we have heard howls of outrage over the casting of 'personalities' from reality television shows such as *Big Brother* in pantomime. Just a year or so back the controversy was over the use of soap stars. Before that, performers from the television show *Gladiators*. Prior to that, sports stars such as Frank Bruno, and back in the 1960s it was the use of the new generation of pop stars which caused outcry. In the 1880s and 1890s, the traditionalists were horrified by the importation of the stars of the Music Hall. 'Is this the end of pantomime as we know it?' was (and is) the cry.

Like so many panto innovations, this one can be traced back to one man. Music Hall stars had appeared in pantos in the provinces and in some of the lesser London theatres already – Nellie Power had appeared as Principal Boy in the 1860s, and G. H. Macdermott played in *Bluebeard* at the Grecian Theatre in 1871. However, it was Augustus Harris who really established the practice. (Later he became Sir Augustus Harris: he was knighted because he was Sheriff of London during a state visit by the Emperor of Germany, not for his contribution to theatre.)

Born in 1852, Harris became manager of Drury Lane in 1879 at the age of 28 – the youngest ever to hold the post – and brought a young man's energy and willingness to experiment to the theatre which had for so long been the principal home of the pantomime. In 1881 he invited Macdermott to play in *Robinson Crusoe*, just the first of many Music Hall stars who were to feature in Drury Lane pantos during his tenure. Thereafter he brought in Marie Lloyd, Herbert Campbell, Little Tich, and the performer who was to have the greatest influence on the development of pantomime since Joseph Grimaldi: Dan Leno.

Harris set out to produce the most spectacular and lavish pantomimes ever seen, and was pretty successful. He used huge casts – for example in *Sinbad the Sailor* there were 500 people on-stage in one scene – and he spent large amounts on costumes and sets. Under Harris's guidance, the transformation scene went, to be replaced by parades which, in some cases, lasted as long as 20 minutes. Typically Victorian in attitude, he intended that these parades should be educational and inspirational. His most famous was of all the English monarchs from William the Conqueror onwards, but others, such as the parade of all Shakespeare's major characters from what Harris considered his most important plays, were equally spectacular and long. However, Harris's thirst for innovation still wasn't satisfied. He was also responsible for setting the idea of a female Principal Boy on a firm footing and, by his encouragement of Dan Leno, for setting the pattern of pantomime Dames that lasts to this day.

The other major change that he made was to make the pantomime

Left: The inimitable Frank Bruno as the Genie in *Aladdin*.

the sole item on the bill. Up to this time, following a tradition more than a century old, pantomimes were afterpieces. At least, nominally they were afterpieces, although as far as the public was concerned they were the main business of the evening.

Harris died at the age of 44, having moved the pantomime a long way in the direction that was to determine its development right up to the present day. He was known as the 'Father of Modern Pantomime' and 'Augustus Druriolanus', for his success in increasing the theatre's reputation.

Why did Harris – and, to be fair, managers of lesser theatres who had, in some cases, anticipated him – bring Music Hall stars into the pantomime? After all, they do seem out of place. E. L. Blanchard established the panto as a more literary medium, following the Victorian taste for the elevated and the educational. Harris himself added to this with his lavish educational parades. So why lower the tone? Why bring in the brashness and, to put no finer point on it, crudeness of the Music Hall?

The answer is because Harris had that other Victorian characteristic: a head for business. Music Hall stars put bums on seats and that was definitely a good thing, for it made sure that pantomime would develop into an entertainment which would cross class boundaries. So let's take a look at ten of those stars and see how they were to influence panto.

G. H. MACDERMOTT (1845–1901)

G. H. Macdermott's importance lay in the fact that he was the first Music Hall star to appear at what was essentially the home of panto, Drury Lane. Born in 1845, he was a sailor, then a bricklayer's labourer before embarking on a stage career. He was best known in his day for the song which epitomizes the attitude we call jingoism:

We won't want to fight
But by jingo if we do,
We've got the ships, we've got the men,
We've got the money too.
We've fought the Bear before
And while Britons shall be true
The Russians shall not have Constantinople!

Above: At over six feet tall and weighing 19 stones, Herbert Campbell was a favourite actor to play the role of a child. Here he is Jack in *Mother Goose*, c. 1903.

(The song, incidentally, refers to Disraeli's hawkish foreign policy, threatening Russia during the Russo–Turkish War of 1877–78.)

HERBERT CAMPBELL (1846–1904)

Herbert Campbell began his career with burnt cork rubbed all over his face as a member of one of the popular minstrel acts of the day. He made his debut in pantomime at the Theatre Royal, Liverpool, in 1871 and first appeared at Drury Lane in 1883. Over six feet tall and weighing more than 19 stones, he was to become, from 1888 until his death, part of a double act with the diminutive Dan Leno, who was to have a major influence on the future of pantomime.

War. He was generally regarded as the best Buttons of his generation.

DAN LENO (1860–1904)

Dan Leno began his stage career as 'Little George, the Infant Wonder, Contortionist and Posturer' at the age of four, using his real name, George Galvin. In 1880 he became Clog Dancing Champion of the World in a competition held in Leeds. His Music Hall career centred around comic songs and monologues, in which he created many popular characters. Mrs Kelly was to form the basis of the role for which he is famous even today – Dame.

Leno first played Dame in *Jack and the Beanstalk* at the Surrey Theatre in 1886. The following year he appeared there again as Tinpanz the Tailor in *Sinbad the Sailor*, however in 1888 Augustus Harris brought him to Drury Lane to play the wicked aunt in *Babes in the Wood*. He stayed there, mainly working as a double act with Herbert Campbell, until his death in 1904. Most of the time he played Dame and, working with writer J. Hickory Wood, developed the role into the one we know today.

In 1901 Leno was summoned to Sandringham to appear before Edward VII. Thereafter he was known as 'the King's Jester'.

Leno and Campbell died within three months of each other in 1904, Campbell as the result of an accident. Having had a nervous breakdown in 1903 – due, it is said, to the pressure of work – Leno died insane.

HARRY LAUDER (1870–1950)

Born in Edinburgh as Henry MacLennan, Sir Harry Lauder was a coalminer for ten years before joining a concert party as an Irish comic, even though he was a Scot. He made his name, however, as a singer/writer of Scottish songs, the most famous being 'Roamin' in the Gloamin". He made his London debut in 1900 and was an overnight sensation, eventually becoming the highest paid British performer of his time.

Lauder was knighted in 1919 for his work organizing entertainment for the troops in the First World

LOTTIE COLLINS (1866–1910)

Like so many Music Hall and panto stars, Lottie Collins was born into a show-business family, although her parentage was, perhaps, one of the oddest: her father was a Jewish blackface minstrel. She began her career at the age of five doing a skipping rope dance and then toured with her sisters Marie and Lizzie as a song-and-dance trio.

In 1891 she became a huge star overnight when she sang what was to become her trademark song, 'Ta-Ra-Ra-Boom-De-Ay' in *Dick Whittington* at the Grand, Islington. From there she went on to become the leading Principal Girl of her time. Incidentally, the song, which is now so closely identified with the London Music Hall, is American. It was a brothel song and the lyrics she sang were somewhat cleaned up.

Her daughter, Jose, followed in the family showbiz tradition and became a star of musical comedy, being best known for playing Theresa in *Maid of the Mountains*.

JENNY HILL (1851–1896)

Quite a number of Music Hall and panto stars ended their lives in less than happy circumstances – Dan Leno's insanity, for instance (see page 46) – but none had such a hard life as Jenny Hill. Her health was so badly broken by her hard life that she died at the early age of 44. Some accounts of Hill's life state that she made her first stage appearance as a singer at the age of seven, but this puts too glamorous a gloss on the reality, which was that she worked at a tavern – the Bradford Tavern – where she had to slave as a cleaner for many hours before beginning her singing.

Hill's nickname was 'The Vital Spark' for her bright and lively stage persona, but this concealed a life of hardship and misery. She married an acrobat,

Opposite: Lottie Collins singing 'Ta-ra-ra-boom-de-ay', the song that became her signature tune.

Right: Little Tich (Harry Relph) wearing his trademark long boots.

who tried to train her to join him in the act and nearly killed her in the process. Then, when she gave birth to her daughter, he left her. In spite of the misery of her private life, she became the leading Principal Boy of her time.

LITTLE TICH (1867–1928)

Just four feet tall when fully grown, Harry Relph got the second part of his stage name, Little Tich, not from his size but from his supposed resemblance, as a young boy, to the Tichborne Claimant, one of the most famous legal cases of the latter half of the nineteenth century.

His solo act, which he was to incorporate into his panto appearances, included comic 'impersonations', where he played a vast range of characters from grocers through soldiers to fairy queens. From 1891 to 1894 he played alongside Dan Leno and other stars in the Drury Lane pantomimes, and he appeared in the very first Royal Command Charity Performance at the Palace Theatre in 1912.

His popularity was not limited to Britain: in 1910 he was made an officer of the Académie Française for services to French theatre.

MARIE LLOYD (1870–1922)

Ask anyone today to name a Music Hall star and the name which is most likely to be remembered is that of Marie Lloyd. Born Matilda Alice Victoria Wood, she was the eldest of 11 children of a waiter and went on to become one of the great names of Music Hall.

In her young days she could be very suggestive, although it was not her material but her delivery that made her so, as one of her most popular songs, 'A Little of What You Fancy Does You Good', shows. But she could also be romantic: 'The Boy I Love Is Up In The Gallery' was to become one of the 'standards' of Music Hall. She played Principal Girl in three pantomimes at Drury Lane: the Princess in *Humpty Dumpty* (1891), Little Red Riding Hood in *Little Bo-Peep, Little Red*

Like so many other performers of the time, he began at a very young age as a singer and player of the penny whistle, then joined a blackface minstrel troupe before going solo in 1884, after his first appearance in pantomime in Glasgow in 1883. While with the minstrel group, Relph perfected what was to become his trademark: a dance in which he balanced on his toes in boots which were almost as long as he was tall.

Above: At the height of her career, Marie Lloyd earned what was for those days a huge sum: £600 a week.

Riding Hood and *Hop o' My Thumb* (1892) (three pantos for the price of one), and Polly Perkins in *Robinson Crusoe* (1893), all with Dan Leno, Herbert Campbell and Little Tich.

It is really quite surprising that Marie Lloyd played Principal Girl even three times, given that she was considered to be somewhat risqué. Later, as she got older, she changed her stage persona and became associated with such songs as 'Oh Mr Porter!', 'My Old Man' and, most tellingly, 'A Bit of a Ruin that Cromwell Knocked About a Bit'.

GEORGE ROBEY (1869–1954)

'The Prime Minister of Mirth' was an unusual Music Hall star. In a field where the cockney reigned supreme, his plummy accent and frequent instruction not to laugh were very different to the norm. He first appeared in panto as one of the babes in *Babes in the Wood* in 1899 and first played Dame (Dame Trott in *Jack and the Beanstalk*) in 1921. Strangely for such a successful Music Hall star, most of his panto appearances were in the provinces.

Like so many other comedians of the period, Robey had his trademark costume: a bowler hat, black coat, hooked stick and thickly painted black eyebrows.

Robey proved to be a very versatile performer and achieved great success at the age of 66 as Falstaff in *Henry IV*, *Part 1* and went on to play the dying Falstaff in Olivier's film of *Henry V*.

He was knighted in the year he died, 1954.

NELLIE WALLACE (1870–1948)

Born in Glasgow, Nellie Wallace, like so many others, began her career as a child performer, which, in her case, was as a clog dancer. She went on to create a stage persona as a moth-eaten, buck-toothed spinster, who wore dilapidated clothes and a ratty piece of fur ('my little bit of vermin'), and became known as 'The Essence of Eccentricity'.

Wallace carried this character over to panto and was the only woman of her time – and one of the very few women ever – to play Dame. In fact, it was the only role in panto she did play, and it was the natural continuance of the character she had created for her Music Hall act.

WORDS, WORDS, WORDS AGAIN!

Augustus Harris and Dan Leno were pivotal figures in the history of pantomime. However, a less well known but equally important person in the development of the genre was Harris's successor, Arthur Collins (1863–1932).

Collins started at Drury Lane as a scenery painter, rose to become Harris's assistant, and then took over from him when he died in 1896. He continued the theatre's commitment to lavish spectacular effects. For example, in an 1899 production of *Jack and the Beanstalk*, he had a chorus of children dressed as soldiers emerging from one of the dead giant's pockets.

But he didn't just preserve the best of what had gone before: he was also an innovator, making major contributions to the development of the genre, moving it much closer to what we know today.

The first was in 1900, when, at the last minute, he booked a writer new to the Lane to draft *The Sleeping Beauty and the Beast*. This was J. Hickory Wood, a former insurance clerk from Manchester, who had written for provincial theatres and for Garrick in London. The show was a success and Wood went on to write for the theatre for the next 12 years. Wood finally got rid of the Harlequinade but, most important of all, he wrote the complete script of *Sleeping Beauty*.

Up to that point there were blank spots in panto scripts which the performers (usually the comics) filled with their own material – something that happens nowadays. Wood, however, worked with Campbell and Leno to produce a script that was tailored to their talents. With a third creative mind working on the gags and relating them to what was happening in the rest of the show, the words assumed as great an importance as they had in Blanchard's

heyday. The consequence was that his pantomimes became very popular, and not just at Drury Lane. In 1913, 33 of Wood's panto scripts were being presented, not only in Britain but right across the British Empire.

A further change that Wood introduced was to restrict the rhyming couplets to the so-called

Right: Arthur Collins, who rose from being a scenery painter to become manager of the Theatre Royal Drury Lane from 1896 to 1924.

Immortals, the Good Fairy and the Demon King and their equivalents. We can thus credit Wood with being the final contributor to the creation of modern pantomime. He took a theatrical form that had, as it were, one foot in the old tradition of the Harlequinade, and created a new form appropriate to the twentieth century – and even the twenty-first.

Collins, like all good theatre managers, was sensitive to public taste and became aware, in the second decade of the twentieth century, that the pantomime audience was ready for a change. He didn't banish the Music Hall stars from Drury Lane's pantomimes, they simply assumed a less important place (except as comics). This was because, in 1912, Collins brought the first of a new group of performers to the genre: the stars of operetta and musical comedy. In *Sleeping Beauty,* Drury Lane's pantomime that year, the Principal Boy was a man, the baritone Wilfred Douthitt. Douthitt returned in 1913 and others of his ilk followed, although it was not long before women went back to playing Principal Boy (at least for the next 40 years).

Thus Collins established, for the first time, the eclectic mix of performers which is characteristic of modern pantomime casts. Musical comedy and Music Hall mixed for the first time, just as today we find pop stars and soap stars rubbing shoulders with sportsmen, straight actors and celebrities. In 1924 Collins retired, by which time the pantomime as we know it was established.

Left: The Principal Girl and the Principal Boy sing one of their duets in *Sleeping Beauty* at the Sunderland Empire in a 1970s production.

Opposite: The extraordinary Vokes family. Standing left to right: Fred and Fawdon; seated left to right: Victoria, Rosina, Jessie. This photograph was taken in 1873.

☆ THE VOKES FAMILY ☆

It can be very much a family thing, theatre. The Redgraves are a particularly good example, with three generations of actors and actresses, and there are two generations of Wests, two of Thaws, two of Dotrices and Pleasances. Then there are groups of siblings, such as the Fienneses and the McGanns. This also happens in the light entertainment world – for example Arthur Askey and his daughter Anthea. Going back into the history of theatre, we have two generations of Riches and three of Grimaldis. However, as a family unit, there was none to compare with the Vokes family.

The family dominated pantomime from 1866 to 1884, particularly at Drury Lane, where they played almost every year from 1869 to 1879. There were five of them altogether, four of whom (Fred, Jessie, Victoria and Rosina) were 'genuine' Vokeses; the fifth member, Walter Fawdon, took the name Vokes when he joined them. Fred's wife, Bella, took over from Rosina when she retired from the group after her marriage in 1879.

They were the children of a theatrical costumier and began their stage careers as The Vokes Children when they were very young. Victoria's first stage appearance was at the age of two and Rosina was a babe in arms. Their first pantomime was at the Lyceum in 1865 in *Humpty Dumpty* and the following year they appeared in the one and only panto by W. S. Gilbert (a pantomime fan): *Harlequin Cock Robin and Jenny Wren; or, Fortunatus and the Water of Life, The Three Bears, The Three Gifts, The Three Wishes, and The Little Man who Woo'd the Little Maid* – a typical example of Gilbertian topsy-turveydom!

Each of the Vokeses had their individual talents. Fred, for example, was famous for his 'eccentric dancing' and was known as 'the man with elastic legs' and Victoria was a highly rated melodrama and 'straight' actress, while all were well known for their singing and acrobatics.

Except for one year when they were on tour, they appeared in the leading roles in every Drury Lane panto between 1869 and 1879, all written by E. L. Blanchard. While initially they were fantastically popular, their appeal began to fade with time, for their act didn't really change. Music Hall artistes could keep the same act for years, as long as they toured the length and breadth of the country and did not keep appearing in the same place, but to do the same in panto simply did not work. When Augustus Harris took over the management of Drury Lane in 1879, after financial disaster struck under the previous manager, F. B. Chatterton, he clearly did not like the Vokeses and they thought he was a tyrant. They left and went to Covent Garden, but when Jessie died in 1884, the group finally broke up.

VARIATIONS ON A THEME

So, we now reach the twentieth century and the modern panto. Surprisingly, for a century that was filled with new developments and innovation in almost every aspect of life, there were no radical changes in pantomime. There was, of course, a steady modification to suit the times, but nothing which changed the genre's direction that was comparable, for example, to the development (or dropping) of the Harlequinade.

The most important change, perhaps, was the decreasing importance of London in panto history. There had been pantos produced in the provinces for many years. Manchester, for example, had its first pantomime in 1743 and Birmingham in 1840. By the 1870s there were so-called 'pantomime trains' running from Manchester and other cities to Leeds for the pantos at the Leeds Grand. The great Augustus Harris spent some time at the Tyne Theatre in Newcastle before moving on to Drury Lane. In Scotland, Glasgow gained a reputation for excellent pantos. In spite of this, London was still the centre of the pantomime world although many London productions, with stars such as Joseph Grimaldi, toured the provinces, attracting huge audiences.

At the start of the twentieth century, this was still the case. Drury Lane, under the management of Collins, was still the undisputed queen of the pantomime world, but another horse was coming up from behind very quickly. The Melville brothers, Walter (1875–1937) and Frederick (1879–1938), took over the Lyceum in 1909 and began to get a good reputation for their pantos. Then, in 1920, for the first time, Drury Lane didn't stage a pantomime. Instead it produced a spectacular drama called *The Garden of Allah* by Robert Hitchens. In fact, panto didn't make a return to Drury Lane until 1929, and then again in 1934. They weren't anywhere near as successful as the theatre's great productions had been

Left: Ian Botham in *Jack and the Beanstalk*, in 1991.

Opposite: Norman Wisdom and Yana in *Turn Again Whittington* at the London Palladium, December 1960. Wisdom began the fashion for male Principal Boys when he played the role in 1956.

Opposite: Cliff Richard as Aladdin – one of the first in a generation of pop stars to appear in pantomime. His backing group, The Shadows, appeared as Wishee, Washee, Poshee and Noshee!

Above: Tommy Steele as Dick Whittington at the London Palladium in 1969. He is generally reckoned to be the best Dick Whittington of the twentieth century.

before and, in any case, the Melvilles's shows at the Lyceum were by now regarded as the best pantos in London. The Melvilles's first panto was in 1910 and the last in 1938, when Frederick died, just a year after the death of his brother. His death was hastened, so it was said, by grief over the loss of Walter.

After the Melvilles it was not until the late 1940s that a clear leader in the pantomime stakes emerged: the London Palladium. The venue was to hold on to its pantomimic pre-eminence until the 1970s, by which time pantomime in the West End was in a state of terminal decline. In the 1960s very few West End theatres could afford the huge costs of a panto (on average around £100,000), and by 1984 there was only one panto playing – in 1992 there was none. A centuries-long tradition came to an end. But, of course, it wasn't the end of pantomime, for hundreds are still produced in theatres, both amateur and professional, throughout the country, including many parts of London. It is just the West End that is a pantomime desert!

At this stage, it seems fitting that we should pause to reflect on some of the major events and contributions made to panto in the second half of the twentieth century.

In 1956 Norman Wisdom played Principal Boy in *Aladdin* at the London Palladium, and set a fashion which was to persist at that theatre, and elsewhere in London, for 15 years. Singers such as Frankie Vaughan, pop stars like Cliff Richard and Tommy Steele, comics like Jimmy Tarbuck and actors like Edward Woodward all played Principal Boy. Then, in 1971, the Palladium cast Cilla Black in the role and the tradition of the female Principal Boy

with its feet. The inevitable backlash came and panto reverted to its previous more innocent self. Interestingly, neither of these changes had much impact in the provinces. I remember at a dress rehearsal at the Sunderland Empire the then director of the theatre, Roy Todds, blasting a comic for trying to introduce blue material. The air became somewhat blue, but the comic got the message!

The 1980s were characterized by the arrival of Australian soap stars in pantos, primarily from *Neighbours* and *Home and Away*. As the popularity of these soaps declined in the 1990s and home-grown soaps replaced them in popular affection, we saw stars of *EastEnders*, *Coronation Street*, *Emmerdale* and the like making appearances, along with the muscle-bound non-actors of *Gladiators*.

It's a little early to be sure, of course, but the current decade shows signs of being the time of the minor celebrity, from reality TV (*Big Brother*'s Jonny Reagan playing in *Aladdin* at the Theatre Royal, Newcastle) or simply being notorious (Neil and Christine Hamilton at Guildford).

One interesting footnote: in 1983 the National Theatre presented its one and only panto, *Cinderella*. Unsurprisingly it wasn't a great success and the experiment was never repeated.

In 1992 pantomime became a National Curriculum subject! Well, that's a bit of an exaggeration, but John Morley's *Dick Whittington* was set for study in English in that year. John Morley, incidentally, is probably the most prolific (and most popular) writer

resumed (with the odd man playing it from time to time – even today).

The 1970s saw a development that did come near to killing panto as a family entertainment. In accordance with the sense of sexual liberation which characterized that decade (and the end of the 1960s), exemplified by shows such as *Oh Calcutta!* and the *Emmanuelle* and *Confessions* films, pantomimes began to get more 'blue'. In particular, the comics began to use more blue material and the family audience began to vote

Opposite: Most mainstream comedians appear in panto, either as Comic or Dame. Here it's Ronnie Corbett as Mother Goose in 1996.

Above: Cilla Black as *Aladdin*. In 1971 she led the return of the female Principal Boy after nearly 20 years of the part being played by men.

of pantomimes. He wrote his first when stationed in Palestine with the Coldstream Guards in 1944, and since then has written well over 200. Many were written for the professional stage but they are extremely popular with amateur groups, and there are usually over 200 amateur productions of his work during most panto seasons.

John Morley brings us back to the second major development in the twentieth century – the amateur pantomime. They aren't new. Charles Dickens, for example, delighted in mounting pantos in his private theatre in his London home, Tavistock House. But the amateur theatre movement, which took off in the late nineteenth century when 'amateur theatricals' were a popular pastime for the middle and upper classes in England, has seized upon panto and made performing it a national pastime.

Drama clubs and amateur operatic and dramatic societies throughout the United Kingdom often fund the rest of their year's programme from the profits of their annual panto. There are societies that do nothing but pantomimes, and many write their own scripts. Panto is still an integral part of the British Christmas.

Surprisingly, amateur pantomimes today are often more adventurous than professional shows. While the professional tend to stick to a very limited number of popular stories, many amateur companies will revive stories that have long been out of favour in the professional theatre world. *Little Red Riding Hood*, *Goldilocks and the Three Bears*, *Ali Baba and the Forty Thieves*, *Puss in Boots*, *The Pied Piper*, *Robinson Crusoe*, *Old King Cole* and *Rumpelstiltskin* have all been produced by amateur groups in the last five years. Amateur companies are also more willing to take liberties with the traditional stories – *The Good, the Bad and the Ugly Sisters*, for example, or *Dick Whittington and Wondercat* – or even pantos created from other well-known stories (which, of course, is in the true tradition of the genre), such as *Dick Turpin*, *King Arthur* or even *Pinocchio*.

London may no longer be the centre of the pantomime world, but there is no doubt that the genre is flourishing as never before.

MODERN PANTOMIME 2

FROM ALADDIN TO TOM THE PIPER'S SON

If someone were to hold a vote to ascertain the most popular pantomime, it would almost certainly be won by *Aladdin* or *Cinderella*. In the 1992–93 professional panto season, each had 30 productions, followed by *Jack and the Beanstalk* and *Dick Whittington* with 20, *Snow White* with 12 and *Babes in the Wood* with 11.

Now let's look at the situation a decade later. Taking a sample of three production companies (for today it is specialist companies that produce the majority of professional pantos), one large, one medium and one small, and looking at their 2002–03 and 2003–04 seasons, *Aladdin* has 15 productions, *Snow White* 14, *Cinderella* 12, *Dick Whittington* 11 and *Jack and the Beanstalk* seven, while *Babes in the Wood* gets only two.

Now, depending on your age, you'll be surprised to see some omissions. Where is *Ali Baba*, or *Sinbad*? Out of favour, I'm afraid, along with many others. If we look at the list of pantos produced professionally since 1880, the range is astonishing – as is the number of those that have vanished almost without trace. The list opposite is not, I hasten to point out, exhaustive.

Can you spot the odd one out?

They are all fairy or folk tales, nursery rhymes or tales from the Arabian Nights except for *Peter Pan*. J. M. Barrie's play about the boy who wouldn't grow up was first performed in 1904 (at the Duke of York's) and quickly established itself as a leading children's Christmas entertainment. In fact, it played at the Duke of York's at Christmas for the next ten years and has rarely been out of London's Christmas repertoire since. Strictly speaking, of course, it isn't a pantomime, but it is so popular that it has come to be regarded as one and some of its characters slightly twisted to fit the panto template. There are, of course, other children's plays that are closely associated with Christmas, such as *Alice in Wonderland*, *The Snow Queen*, *A Christmas Carol*, *Treasure Island*, *The Lion, the Witch and the Wardrobe* and, more recently, *The Snowman*, but none of them have joined *Peter Pan* in receiving pantomime status.

Page 64: Linda Lusardi and Stu Francis in *Snow White and the Seven Dwarfs*. The ex-page three girl has become a panto regular as Principal Girl.

Left: J. M. Barrie, whose *Peter Pan* has always been a favourite Christmas play. As soon as his copyright expired, it became a pantomime.

Opposite: A modern-day *Peter Pan* production.

☆ POPULAR SHOWS ☆

Aladdin	Ali Baba and the Forty Thieves
Babes in the Wood	Beauty and the Beast
Bluebeard	Dick Whittington
Goldilocks and the Three Bears	Goody Two-Shoes
Hansel and Gretel	Hop o' My Thumb
The House that Jack Built	Humpty-Dumpty
Jack and the Beanstalk	Jack the Giant Killer
Jack and Jill	Little Bo-Peep
Little Jack Horner	Little Miss Muffett
Little Red Riding Hood	Mother Goose
Old King Cole	Old Mother Hubbard
Peter Pan	The Pied Piper
Puss in Boots	The Queen of Hearts
Robinson Crusoe	Rumpelstiltskin
Sinbad the Sailor	Sleeping Beauty
Snow White and the Seven Dwarfs	Tom the Piper's Son
The White Cat	

There are 33 in all and they are just the ones that were popular.

THERE'S NOTHING LIKE A DAME

Thank goodness! Can you imagine how fearsome a creature such a character would be in real life? Loud and vulgar, with no dress sense; domineering; incompetent at whatever her job might be – mother, washerwoman, cook; always broke but with a wide range of outfits, all in appallingly bad taste; vain and cunning but with the proverbial heart of gold. Oh yes, and on the hunt for a man, any man. That's the Dame!

Somehow or other she has come to dominate the modern pantomime. Where once Harlequin then the Clown was the main figure, now it's that man in a woman's clothing, the Dame. A man playing a woman, of course, is not something unusual in British theatrical tradition. We all know that women in the plays of Shakespeare's time were played by boys. It goes back even further to the comic women's parts in the Mysteries, such as Mrs Noah, which were played by men. There is no doubt that the origin of the Betty in the Morris Dance stretches back to the simple morality plays of the Middle Ages. Women were not allowed to appear on the stage until the late seventeenth century.

It has been suggested that, even after women were allowed to appear, actresses didn't want to play such parts because they were not glamorous. But this doesn't stand up. Do we take it that, for example, Mrs Malaprop would be played by a man, or that a woman would choose to play Juliet but not the Nurse? What about that bitter harridan in *Richard III*, Queen Margaret? Would women refuse to play her but insist on playing Lady Anne? No, the reason that men have played the Dame from as early as 1731, when Harper played the Cook in *Dick Whittington*, is because it's funnier. Old Mother Reilly would never have got the laughs 'she' did if we hadn't known it was Arthur Lucan playing her. And if Lily Savage was really a woman, we wouldn't laugh a quarter as much as we do. Like all humour, it's impossible to explain. We all know that having to explain a joke kills it stone dead, and so it is with the pantomime Dame: the fact that it is a man just makes the character funny. It is interesting that on the few occasions women have played the part, the slapstick element, particularly the 'slosh' scenes and the custard pies, was played down and that the only successful female Dame, Nellie Wallace ('The Essence of Eccentricity'), played a caricature of a woman, which is the point of the Dame.

Left: Ronné Coyles in a traditional 'glam' pose as Dame at the Sunderland Empire in the 1970s.

Opposite: Simon Bashford as Mother Goose. The exaggerated make-up and the attempt to look girlish is a typical Dame characteristic.

WIDOW TWANKEY

Probably the best-known Dame is Widow Twankey, Aladdin's mother. She was originally, in the Covent Garden production of 1813, called Widow Ching Mustapha, a name which is a strange mixture of Muslim and Chinese – typically pantomime. It was H. J. Byron who first used her modern name in 1861. It was a contemporary reference that has stuck, unlike the majority of such references which die when the event that gave them birth is forgotten. Twankey comes from Twankay Tea, a fashionable brand in 1861, which came from the Chinese province of Tuan Ky (or Twan Kay). She was originally the widow of a tailor but, by the middle of the nineteenth century, she had become a washerwoman, and it is this trade, with all its opportunities for jokes, 'slosh' scenes and sight-gags, which has become established in the modern pantomime.

DAME DURDEN/DAME TROT

The names of the Dames do change over the years. Jack's mother in *Jack and the Beanstalk*, for instance, was called Dame Durden when the panto made its first appearance as *Jack and the Beanstalk; or, Harlequin and the Ogre* at Drury Lane in 1819 and she still had that name when Dan Leno played her (in his first performance as Dame) at the Surrey Theatre in 1886. A little later, however, when Leno played the part at Drury Lane, she was Mrs Simpson one time and Dame Trot another. In the Drury Lane production of 1910–11, when played by George Graves, she became Mrs Halleybutt (halibut: get it?).

For the modern audience, however, Jack's mother is Dame Trot. Although some less sensitive comics have been known to point out how close the name is to 'the trots' (as in diarrhoea). In fact the word 'trot' was eighteenth-century slang for the vagina, which somehow by the nineteenth century had come to mean an old hag.

COOK

The Dame in *Dick Whittington* has always been the Cook, at least as far back as 1731. Thomas Greenwood called her Dame Dorothy Drippington in 1852, but she is usually known as Sarah the Cook.

THE UGLY SISTERS

The Dame in *Cinderella* is interesting. Today there are two, the Ugly Sisters (known in the business as the

'Uglies'), but in some earlier versions of the story Cinderella had a wicked stepmother who treated her as the Uglies do today. They made their first appearance as Cinderella's (not ugly) stepsisters in Rossini's opera *La Cenerentola* (1817), where they are called Clorinda and Tisbe (anglicized to Thisbe in panto). They appeared as unkind and selfish stepsisters in *Harlequin and Cinderella; or, The Little Glass Slipper* at Covent Garden in 1820, but were first introduced into pantomime as the Uglies in H. J. Byron's 1860 Extravaganza *Cinderella; or, The Lover, the Lackey, and the Little Glass Slipper* at the Royal Strand Theatre.

The Ugly Sisters have had more names than any other characters in pantomime history. Each writer seems to exercise his ingenuity to produce suitable ones: Namby and Pamby, Tutti and Frutti, Valderma and Germolena (one of my favourites), Pearl and Deane, Hilda and Tilda, Posh and Scary, Britney and Cher, Dannii and Kylie, Ammonia and Amnesia … the list goes on.

OTHER MAIN DAMES

As in *Cinderella*, the Dame in *Sleeping Beauty* has changed over the years. Originally the Dame was the Cook (a part once played by Sir Henry Irving – early in his career, of course!), but modern-day versions of the panto have the Nurse in the role. In some pantomimes the Dame is the eponymous character. *Mother Goose* and *Old Mother Hubbard* are obvious examples of this. Incidentally, the original Mother Goose role was an old crone; it

Opposite: Dancer and choreographer Wayne Sleep, who was once principal dancer with the Royal Ballet, appears here as the colourful Dame Foxy Trot in *Jack and the Beanstalk*, in 2001.

Right: Andrew Ryan regularly appears as Dame at the Kenneth More Theatre, in Ilford.

was the ubiquitous Dan Leno who created the modern version at Drury Lane in 1902.

MANUFACTURING A DAME ROLE

There are some pantos where the original story does not have a dame or even a suitable character to make into one, so writers have been forced to invent. In *Little Red Riding Hood,* for example, the grandmother has been used. Then there's Mrs Crusoe (Robinson Crusoe's mother, not his wife). In fact, bringing in a mother character is probably the obvious way to introduce a Dame. Another example is in *Sinbad the Sailor.*

Above: Les Dawson as Sarah the Cook in *Dick Whittington*, in 1991. His Dames were based on the television pieces 'Cissie and Ada' that he did with Roy Barraclough.

Opposite: Douglas Byng as the Queen in *Sleeping Beauty*, in 1944–5. Byng's Dames, he claimed, were all 'real characters' – but they were also very camp!

Probably the panto that provides the greatest challenge to the writer is *Goldilocks and the Three Bears*. Where is the Dame there? Prolific panto writer John Morley got round that one by having the three bears join a circus which is managed by the (incompetent) Dame.

Dames may seem to be the same but, as John Inman says, they each have a character of their own. It isn't enough simply to put on a frock. Of course, each performer brings his own touches, some of which are remembered and picked up by his successors. Les Dawson, for example, owed much of the Dames he created – for each performer creates the part anew – to Norman Evans. Ada, the television character he created for the 'Cissie and Ada' interludes with Roy Barraclough became the basis of his Dame performances, and in many ways resembled Evans's Fanny Fairbottom.

GEORGE LACY (1904–89)

George Lacy first played Dame when he was 24 and carried on doing so in over 60 pantos, making his last appearance when he was 80. All who saw him perform, speak of his skill and talent; however, Lacy's longest-lasting contribution was the fact that he was the first Dame to change his costume in every scene, each 'frock' getting more and more extravagant and silly. On one spectacular occasion he appeared in a dress made to look like a snooker table, with green baize, pockets, balls and cues!

THE GREATEST DAMES

But of course it was Dan Leno who had the greatest effect on the development of the Dame, for not only did he redirect the focus of the panto from the Clown to the Dame, he essentially created the part. There had been Dames before, of course. Grimaldi had played the part in his boy-hood, but in his day they were minor characters, old crones that were good for up-and-coming young performers, as Grimaldi was at that time, to cut their teeth on. What Leno did was to change the part from a stock figure to a realistic character – or as realistic a character as you can get in a pantomime. When Leno first set foot on the Surrey Theatre stage as Dame Durden in 1886, the primacy of the Clown was over and the Dame took centre stage.

If John Lun (Rich) was the greatest Harlequin and Grimaldi was the greatest Clown, who earns the accolade of the greatest Dame?

Clearly Leno must be in the running, for he was so enormously influential, virtually creating the part. But when Rich/Lun died, there was never another

Above: Norman Evans performing an 'Over the Garden Wall' monologue as his most famous character, Fanny Fairbottom.

Opposite: 'Big-hearted' Arthur Askey (or 'Big-hearted Martha', as he was called when a Dame) as the Nurse in *Babes in the Wood*, c. 1950s.

Harlequin to compare with him, and no one ever measured up to Grimaldi as Clown. Not even his own son did, which was a great disappointment to him, for, like all fathers, he had hoped that he would carry on the family business. In fact, between his retirement and his death, what with his injuries and poor health and the disappointment with his son, when asked how he was, Grimaldi would answer, 'Grim all day!' But the departure of Dan Leno from the pantomime scene did not herald the end of the importance of the Dame. On the contrary, he had created the foundations on which others would build … which means there are many contenders for the title. Here are just a few.

DOUGLAS BYNG (1893–1987)

Douglas Byng was regarded as one of the greatest Dames of the 1920s and 1930s and actually appeared in the part 27 times. He also appeared in cabaret and revue – he topped the bill in the Cochran revues from 1925 to 1931 – and was acclaimed for his sophistication, which essentially meant that he was very camp. He wasn't always subtle. In his comic song 'I'm One of the Queens of England' he

sang, 'One thing is certain, I'm not the Virgin Queen', which was something quite daring for the time. He rejected the idea that he was just a drag queen. 'My women were all characters,' he once said. After his death, one journalist wrote that he should have been honoured with the DLE – Dame of the Liverpool Empire!

NORMAN EVANS (1901–62)

In 1943 Norman Evans was playing Dame in *Humpty Dumpty* at the Alhambra in Bradford and sitting in the audience was a seven-year-old boy who was so inspired by Evans's performance that he decided there and then he wanted to be an actor. That was Edward Petherbridge, who was to go on to become a member of Olivier's National

Theatre company at the Old Vic, a founder member of the Actors' Company and a member of the Royal Shakespeare Company. Edward Woodward, whose acting career went in a different direction to Petherbridge's, also cites Evans, whom he saw at the Croydon Empire, as one of those who inspired him to go into theatre.

Like most pantomime Dames, Norman Evans (who was actually discovered in his home town of Rochdale by no less a star than Gracie Fields) played the variety halls where he was known mainly for his 'Over the Garden Wall' monologues as Fanny Fairbottom (which he also performed on radio). Fanny's ample bosom would bash against the wall when she slipped – 'That's twice on the same brick this week!' she would cry. It was Fanny whom he played as Dame to great acclaim until just before he died in 1962.

DIFFERENT APPROACHES TO BEING DAME

There are three distinct approaches to playing Dame. There's the style perfected by Leno and carried on by, for example, Arthur Lucan. Their Dames were realistic – clearly a man but believable as a woman. This is not an approach used much in the modern pantomime, although I would suggest that, perhaps, Nicholas Parsons comes fairly close to it, and certainly Jack Tripp (who retired in 2000 after a panto career stretching back to the 1940s) was firmly part of that tradition. Then there's the usual modern approach, where the fact that the performer is a man is obvious. Norman Evans and Les Dawson typify that approach, as, to be honest, do most Dames today, both amateur and professional.

DANNY LA RUE (1928–)

It is a far cry from Norman Evans to the man whom Bob Hope called 'the most glamorous woman in the world' – Danny La Rue. In fact, he more or less invented the drag queen style. He is a female impersonator, not simply a man playing a woman's part in a situation, such as panto, where it is expected. For example, he played Dolly Levi in *Hello Dolly* at the West End's Prince of Wales Theatre in the early 1980s and took it very seriously indeed. He does not, he says, try to send up women. He does his best to be respectful. And he does emphasize that 'when people come to see Danny La Rue, they come to see glamour'.

Left: Billy Dainty et al at the Wolverhampton Grand, in 1972. Dainty was a classically trained actor who became one of the twentieth century's greatest Dames.

Oddly enough, Danny La Rue's career, which has led to the acceptance of the female impersonator in mainstream entertainment, has helped create another type of Dame, exemplified by Lily Savage (Paul O'Grady). It is too early to say whether this more earthy type of Dame will last. It may well be a one-off. We shall see. But that's what's so great about pantomime and about the Dame character in particular: it adapts and changes according to the times.

ARTHUR ASKEY (1900–82)
Like Norman Evans and Les Dawson, Arthur Askey didn't use much in the way of make-up. He wasn't trying to be a woman, he was pretending to be a woman and audiences knew what to expect from him. He would greet them with his catchphrase, 'Hello playmates!' and you could be certain that 'Ey thang yew' would occur innumerable times. Audiences would also expect one of his silly songs and 'The Bee Song' would be greeted with rapturous applause ('Buzz, buzz, buzz, buzz / Busy bee, busy bee / Buzz if you like / But don't sting me!'). Most 'Great Dames' specialize in the part, but 'Big-hearted Arthur' (who, in fact, was small – hence the name) also played other parts in his long career. His Buttons was highly regarded and he played many other of the comic roles. However, it was as 'Big-hearted Martha' that he had his greatest success.

BILLY DAINTY (1927–86)
Billy Dainty played Dame for 30 years and created his own style, based on a repertoire of eccentric dancing and funny walks. He was a fine dancer and actor. He trained at the RADA (Royal Academy of Dramatic Art) and, while he was there, became a pupil of Buddy Bradley, who choreographed for Fred Astaire.

One of his most popular dance routines was a 'cod' ballet in which he dressed in a tutu, but it is for the funny walks that he is best remembered.

In 2002 I was reviewing a touring production of *Tartuffe* in which actor David Tarkenter, playing the grandmother Madame Pernelle, would sweep across the stage with darting hen-like upper-body movements. In the interval, eavesdropping on the audience (as any good critic should), if I heard 'Isn't he like Billy Dainty?' once, I heard it a hundred times.

When he died, Dainty's obituary in *The Stage* said that he had 'a unique style that owed nothing to anybody', and that really did sum him up. He fully deserves his place among the 'Great Dames'.

JOHN INMAN

In the 2002–03 panto season, John Inman, star of the legendary television sitcom Are You Being Served? *appeared in one of his favourite roles, Widow Twankey, in* Aladdin.

As you listen to John talking about pantomime, one thing emerges very clearly: here is a man who is passionate about the subject.

'It's an art form of its own,' he insists. 'It has its own style and energy. It takes far more energy to do a panto than a play.'

Inman has done more than 40 pantos and has loved every one. He has played Buttons, Wishee Washee and even Aladdin in the past but Dame is his favourite role.

'Dame is good for both laughs and pathos,' he says, with obvious relish. 'I've played 15 Mother Gooses, five Widow Twankeys and seven Ugly Sisters. I've also played Dame Trot in *Jack* and Nurse in *Babes in the Wood*. But I don't just put a frock on,' he says. 'To me, they're all different. They each have a character of their own.'

Does this mean that he prepares like an actor?

'Oh no. I'm not sure that pantomime has anything to do with acting,' he replies. 'You see, pantomime is not really written: it's remembered. There's a whole range of scenes, gags and sketches that aren't written down. If you look at the script for *Aladdin*, for example, you'll find big gaps with just the words "John's material"!'

What does he think of the use of performers from other fields being used in panto?

'Well,' he said quite seriously, 'I promise Ian Botham I'll not play cricket and I promise Frank Bruno I won't take up boxing.' He grins, but it's quite obvious that he is very serious. It puts bums on seats, but he clearly is not happy with it.

'We've been fortunate', he says, 'that Jonny [Jonny Regan, one of the *Big Brother* contestants who was appearing with him in *Aladdin* and who, although a fireman, has also played the North East working men's clubs as a singer] knows what he's doing.'

One of the difficulties and joys of pantomime is the wide range of ages in the audience. You've got to please everybody. 'It's not just the kids. You have to keep the adults happy, too. You please the kids by telling the story – and by not mucking it about either. They want the proper story. Then you please the adults with the other ingredients. But they mustn't get in the way of the story. Sometimes the story needs to be very carefully told. In *Aladdin* we have the magic lamp and the magic ring, and you've got to be very careful to make sure the children don't get confused. So you can't muck about with the story.'

The days when each theatre produced its own panto are gone and now the big shows are produced centrally by companies such as Qdos, the producers of *Aladdin*. Does this not make it difficult to localize the show?

'Not at all. It's really always been left to the individual. How could you do a pantomime in Newcastle and not mention Newcastle United? You do a little research and find out the names of local personalities, and you just work them into the show. But you don't make a big thing of it. Localizing is only a small part of the show.'

How does it work? How long is the rehearsal period, for example?

'Ten days. We start off in London. Sometimes the cast's together but for a great deal of the time we work separately on each bit of the show. Then we come together and integrate everything. Then we'll do two days at the theatre to integrate the Babes, who've been learning their routines at home, and pull the whole thing together with the technical crew and so on.'

And after all these years, does he still enjoy it?

'Oh yes! As long as I keep working, I'll do panto. I love it!'

OH BOY!

The Principal Boy in a pantomime is traditionally played by a girl but, contrary to popular belief, the idea of women playing men did not originate with panto.

The first known Principal Boy – an unknown actress in *Harlequin and Fortunio* in 1815 – was far from the first to play what was called a 'breeches part'. Seventy-five years earlier an actress by the name of Margaret (Peg) Woffington played Sir Henry Wildair in Farquhar's *The Constant Couple*, and, of course, we are all familiar with the opera convention of a woman (usually an alto) playing a young man. The best-known example is probably Cherubino in Mozart's *The Marriage of Figaro*, but many will also be familiar with Prince Orlovsky in Strauss's *Die Fledermaus*.

The first named Principal Boy we know of was Eliza Povey (1804–61), who played Jack in the 1819 Drury Lane pantomime *Jack and the Beanstalk; or, Harlequin and the Ogre*. However, she had to have a double for the stunts. Women were not

supposed to be able to handle anything requiring physical dexterity, and so the actor Jack Bologna (1781–1846), who was the regular Harlequin at Sadler's Wells and Covent Garden and who had played alongside Grimaldi, had to climb the beanstalk instead of her, and he took over from her completely in the Harlequinade, because women could not be expected to be acrobatic.

The biggest influence on the development of the Principal Boy as a part for a woman was Madame Vestris (1797–1856), who was a singer, actress, producer and theatre manager (see page 41). She ran the Olympic Theatre at which she produced (and appeared in) Planché's Extravaganzas. In 1820 she played Don Giovanni in the Extravaganza *Giovanni in London* and went on to play Macheath in *The Beggar's Opera* at the Haymarket. Then, in 1837, she played her first pantomime Principal Boy, Ralph in *Puss in Boots*, where she did for the first time what has become the Principal Boy's trademark even today (although now it is done as a joke) – she slapped her thigh! As to why she did it – patience, we're coming to that.

The first specialist in the part that we know of was Lydia Thompson (1836–1908), who made her first appearance as Principal Boy at the Lyceum at the age of 25. It was Augustus Harris whose influence really established the role when he cast Ada Blanche (1862–1953) as Little Boy Blue in *Little Bo-Peep, Little Red Riding Hood and Hop o' My Thumb*. In fact, he cast her as Principal Boy from 1892 to 1897.

So why did Madame Vestris slap her thigh? To draw attention to her legs, of course! The Victorian Age was a prudish one and so the only way that men could get a look at women's legs, outside of

Left: Ada Blanche as Robinson Crusoe, in 1893. Blanche was one of those actresses who, although popular, never quite achieved star status.

Opposite: Jean Kent as Prince Charming, featured on the cover of *Illustrated*, in January 1948. Kent started her career as a chorus girl at the Windmill Theatre and became a star of British films in the 40s and 50s.

WEEK ENDING JANUARY 17 1948

EVERY WEDNESDAY THREEPENCE

ILLUSTRATED

PRINCE CHARMING

marriage or 'houses of ill-repute', was onstage when they were playing the parts of men and wearing tights. So her thigh-slapping was in effect saying, 'Come on, boys. Have a good look!' This says something very important about the Principal Boy: we are not to think of 'him' as a boy at all. 'He' is a shapely young woman and the Victorians liked their women shapely: the waif-like figure of the modern supermodel would have horrified them. By playing the part of a man, the Principal Boy was retaining, or even emphasizing, her femininity. The women who played the part were emphatically not male impersonators, even though Vesta Tilley was one of them.

This is all rather odd, for the character of the Principal Boy is at odds with 'his' appearance. 'He' is brave and bold, and not a little chauvinistic. His lover, the Principal Girl, is the little woman who must be protected. But then no one ever said that panto had to be logical.

This rather ambiguous situation – female body with a male temperament – makes it an easy role for men to take over. A female Dame seems somehow wrong, even though it has been done in the past, but we easily accept a male Principal Boy. That change first happened as early as the beginning of the last century when, between 1912 and 1915, Drury Lane booked male operetta stars to play Principal Boy. It happened again in the 1950s and 1960s when, following Norman Wisdom's success in the role, pop stars, comedians and even straight actors ruled supreme. As we've already seen, Frankie Vaughan, Cliff Richard, Tommy Steele, Jimmy Tarbuck and even Edward Woodward all took on the role. In 1971, however, Cilla Black played Principal Boy at the London Palladium and the old tradition was revived. Today, we find men taking the role almost as often as women – except in amateur productions where, perhaps inevitably, companies prefer to stick with tradition.

young actresses at the start of their careers. It is hardly a demanding part and probably not terribly satisfying to the majority of actresses. It was a long time before the Principal Girl got to do any funny lines and even in these more liberated times she tends to be the straight character in gags.

LOTTIE COLLINS

Lottie Collins was one of the Victorian age's leading Principal Girls. She started her Music Hall career at the age of 15, had her greatest pantomime hit when she was 25 and continued to play the role into her thirties. Her contemporary Marie Lloyd made her first appearance at the age of 21. Although, not being terribly well-suited to the role, she only played it at Drury Lane three times, from 1891 to 1893.

There is not a long list of well-known names who have regularly played Principal Girl as there is for other panto roles, and the majority don't play it more than once or twice. But as always there are exceptions to the rule.

JULIE ANDREWS

Julie Andrews, for example, played Principal Girl four times, although her first appearance at the age of 13

in the 1948–49 season was as Humpty Dumpty. In 1951 she played Red Riding Hood alongside Tony Hancock; in 1951–52 it was Princess Badroubaldour in *Aladdin*; the following year she moved to the Coventry Hippodrome where she played Princess Bettina in *Jack and the Beanstalk* (with Norman Wisdom); and finally in 1953–54 she played Cinders in *Cinderella* at the London Palladium alongside Spike Milligan and Eric Sykes.

Among those who have played Principal Girl rather more recently are Twiggy, singer Mary Hopkin, Dana, Linda Lusardi, Melinda Messenger, Julie Buckfield, Michaela Strachan, Sophie Lawrence and numerous soap stars from both the UK and Australia.

For many it's their first stage role, moving from a soap or – increasingly commonly – from children's television. Children's TV presenters are a good bet for Principal Girl roles. They may have no theatre track record and the adults may not know who they are, but the kids do and they're keen to see in the flesh someone who has become, as it were, a 'friend' on television. After all, pantos are for kids – or so they tell us.

MAKE 'EM LAUGH!

There are many opportunities for comics in panto, but there's always one who stands out, who talks to the audience, in whose 'gang' all the children want to be. He's often the Dame's son. In four pantos he has a traditional name that stretches back to the nineteenth century. He is Buttons in *Cinderella*, Wishee Washee in *Aladdin*, Idle Jack in *Dick Whittington* and Simple Simon in *Jack and the Beanstalk*. The man who plays the part is in a direct line of descent from Grimaldi.

He is usually the hero's, or in *Cinderella* the heroine's, best friend – and the audience's. His first action when he comes on stage is usually to call out 'Hiya kids!' or something of that nature. He's never satisfied with the loudness of their response and makes them shout again and again until they are screaming at the tops of their voices. This 'lesson' is reinforced at regular intervals during the show! He will also involve the children in the show, asking them to watch something important he leaves at the side of the stage or to let him know when a particular character appears. This, of course, is another opportunity for the kids to scream their heads off

because they have to try it and the first few times he can't hear them. '[So and so] can't hear you!' becomes the signal for unbridled noise-making.

Every pantomime has its Comic or Clown, who is still sometimes called the 'Joey' in honour of Grimaldi. Let's take a look at a few of the more famous ones.

BUTTONS

Buttons, Cinderella's best friend, is a page, hence the name. He is called after the row of buttons down the front of the traditional pageboy's costume. But he wasn't always called Buttons. He was given that name by H. J. Byron back in 1860 in *Cinderella; or, The Lover, the Lackey and the Little Glass Slipper*. When Grimaldi played the role in 1820, he was called Pedro but he has had many other names. Clowns, we are told, are sad creatures and Buttons fits the picture, for in most modern pantos he is in love with Cinderella. He knows that his love is hopeless and so, unselfishly, he helps her to be reunited with Prince Charming, the man she loves. A bittersweet victory from his point of view and offering plenty of chances for 'ahs' from the audience.

Cinderella remains one of the most popular pantomimes and the roll call of comics who have played the part is impressive and includes Arthur Askey, John Inman, Roy Hudd, Rolf Harris, Des O'Connor, Tommy Steele and David Jason. David Jason, in fact, has only played in one panto and that was *Cinderella* at the Theatre Royal, Newcastle, with Leah Bell (local heroine!) playing Cinders. He was

Left: David Jason in his one and only panto, as Buttons in *Cinderella* at the Theatre Royal, Newcastle.

Opposite: A fabulous combination – Arthur Askey and Cliff Richard in *Aladdin* at the London Palladium in 1964.

Above: Hale and Pace in *Dick Whittington* in 2002–3.

Opposite: 'If it'll get a laugh!' might be panto's motto, even if it *is* a fox. And Basil Brush certainly got the laughs in *Dick Whittington* at the Sunderland Empire.

very nervous but came alive once there was an audience. He did have an unpleasant experience, however. He was supposed to fly across the stage at one point and not only was the harness very uncomfortable, even painful, but control was lost, he bumped into the scenery and was left dangling in mid-air. This was at the dress rehearsal: the flying did not make it to the first night. How do I know? I was there. I was working at the theatre at the time and I can tell you that I winced in sympathy.

WISHEE WASHEE
The pantomime that bids fair to being *the* most popular nowadays is *Aladdin* and in this panto the Clown is Wishee Washee. He is always Widow Twankey's assistant in the laundry and most often he is Aladdin's

brother (Aladdin, of course, being the Principal Boy). He was a late addition to the cast of the show, appearing first in 1889 and becoming a regular after Dan Leno played him at Drury Lane in 1896. The laundry provides many opportunities for sight-gags and slapstick (how many Chinese Policemen have been put through the mangle?) and so comics love the part. In the 1950s, during the period of popularity of the male Principal Boy, Cliff Richard played Aladdin, but there were suddenly four Wishee Washees: Wishee, Washee, Noshee and Poshee, who were played by The Shadows.

IDLE JACK
Dick Whittington isn't so popular nowadays, but its Clown, Idle Jack, has been played by a regular who's who of comedians, with Ken Dodd, Frankie Howerd and Jimmy Tarbuck being among the most notable.

SIMPLE SIMON
As in *Aladdin*, there is often no place for the comic in the original story, so a character is often imported from elsewhere. Such is the case with *Jack and the Beanstalk* where the clown, Simple Simon, came from the nursery rhyme 'Simple Simon', which has formed the basis of the odd panto or two in the past. As a panto *Simple Simon* was not terribly popular, but one suspects that producers didn't like to see a good clown character go to waste and so decided that he would fit into *Jack and the Beanstalk* quite nicely.

TINBAD THE TAILOR
Another pantomime that doesn't get many outings nowadays is *Sinbad the Sailor*. It is, perhaps, a little more fluid, a little less set in its ways, than many other shows, but traditionally its Clown is called Tinbad the Tailor, an obvious play on words. This might not even be worth mentioning except for the fact that it was in this part that Dan Leno made his panto debut in 1886 at the Surrey Theatre. He changed the name of the character to Tinpanz the Tailor. Incidentally, the name of that panto, *Sinbad and the Little Old Man of the Sea; or, The Tinker, the Tailor, the Soldier, the Sailor, the Apothecary, Ploughboy, Gentleman and Thief*, hardly trips off the tongue, does it?

☆ ANYTHING FOR A LAUGH! ☆

Traditionally, a pantomime has a Clown; nowadays a Comic or comedian. But laughter is so important a part of panto that other comic characters have crept in over the years. Some have become so well-established that we cannot imagine the panto without them. Where would *Aladdin* be without the Chinese Policemen or *Cinderella* without the Broker's Men?

Many of the standard panto gags actually require a number of comic characters. Take the Awkward Squad, for instance. As we know, pantos involve a fight against evil and so sometimes one of the characters – often, but not invariably, the Dame – decides that the forces of good need to be drilled like soldiers, so (s)he lines up the Comic, the Principal Boy and . . . who else is there? With an extra Comic or two, we can have a hilarious scene in which every bit of drill goes completely wrong – in numerous ways. Chorus members can, of course, be used, but they're normally dancers and singers, not actors or Comics, so to have at least one (preferably two) additional comic character gives much greater flexibility.

Sometimes one of the extra Comics will be the baddie's sidekick (see page 92). But what on earth is the baddie's sidekick doing helping the goodies? Well, he could be acting as a spy or he could just be brought into these scenes because he knows how to be funny – no one could ever accuse pantomime of being a slave to consistency or logic. The advantage of having two extra Comics, of course, is that it allows the producers to book double acts: Morcambe and Wise, Cannon and Ball, Little and Large, the Chuckle Brothers, Maxie and Mitch – the list of double acts that have played panto is long. And there's a further advantage: they come with ready-made material that can easily be slotted into the plot.

THE FAIRY AND THE RAT

Pantomimes are about the struggle between good and evil: sometimes the evil is domestic nastiness (the Ugly Sisters), sometimes it is pure and unadulterated (the Demon King). Good is usually represented by a fairy (for example, the Fairy Godmother in *Cinderella*) – a supernatural character – whereas bad can be supernatural (Demon King), animal (King Rat) or human (Abanazar).

The Good Fairy always enters stage right (which is the audience's left) and the baddie stage left, because for centuries the left (in Latin: *sinister*) has always been regarded as, at best, unlucky or, at worst, evil. The Good Fairy will be lit in a warm or open white spotlight, whereas the character occupying the evil spot will be lit in green.

The use of these symbolic characters to represent the struggle which lies at the heart of the panto goes back many centuries. The Morality Plays of the Middle Ages represented good and evil onstage. However, over 1,500 years before, the Greek tragedian Euripides had introduced the *deus ex machina*, the 'god from the machine' (so called because he was lowered onto the stage by a crane from the top of the skéné, the building which stood at the back of the stage). He made his appearance out of the blue at the end of the play in order to solve the problems facing the characters and make sure that good triumphed.

A later development was the Benevolent Agent, who brought the opening of the early pantomimes to an end and signalled the beginning of the Harlequinade via the transformation scene. This Benevolent Agent was usually female (although the part may have been played by a man) and was often a fairy or a figure from mythology. She would usually appear again later to untangle the problems faced by the lovers – usually by a wave of her magic wand – and carry them off to the Bower of Bliss where they could live happily ever after. And, of course, the fairy stories that so influenced the development of pantomime have their magical characters whose function it was to guide and protect the hero/heroine.

An obvious influence must have been the Gothic novel – indeed, the whole Gothic movement, which included poetry and the visual arts as well as the novel, and which had its heyday from around 1760 to possibly even as late as 1890. This period saw the publication of Walpole's *The Castle of Otranto* (1764), Lewis's *The Monk* (1796) and Mary Shelley's *Frankenstein* (1818). A very weighty background for two pantomime characters who confront each other across the stage in front of the curtain and speak in rhyming couplets, while the audience cheers one and boos and hisses the other. But that's the nature of panto: it may be very much 'of the people' and not, by any stretch of the imagination, high art, but it is the product of more than 1,000 years of artistic history and still shows the signs, even today.

Above: Dame Anna Neagle as the Fairy Godmother in *Cinderella* at the London Palladium in 1985 (a year before she died).

We've already mentioned the Fairy Godmother in *Cinderella*, but what other 'goodie' supernatural characters are there?

Good fairies all! Dressed in white with magic wands, they glide through pantos in a shower of glitter dust bringing peace and love and we are never in doubt that they will win. Although sometimes we have, I feel, a sneaking hope that they won't, because they are far less interesting than the evil characters. Somehow they never make quite the same impact as the baddies, nor are there as many varieties. Just look at the range of baddies: the wicked fairy Carabosse in *Sleeping Beauty*; the Demon King in *Mother Goose*; King Rat in *Dick Whittington*; Abanazar in *Aladdin*; Captain Hook in *Peter Pan*. Give actors the choice and they'll play the baddie every time. In fact, in recent years, these roles have been the choice of 'real' actors. Anyone who has seen Brian Blessed playing Captain Hook can have no doubt whatsoever of the enjoyment such a part can bring to an actor.

Sometimes these characters, good and bad, are called the Immortals. It's a bit of a misnomer in that some of them (Hook, for example, and Abanazar) are not supernatural, just wonderfully evil humans. But it's a tradition going back to the nineteenth century and so the name sticks.

Very occasionally an Immortal will appear well on in the show and is neither good nor bad, just very powerful. The obvious example is the Genie of the Lamp (and his occasional companion, the Genie of the Ring) in *Aladdin*. One Genie is obviously needed, but two? It could be thought to be a plot necessity, but just think who plays the Genie nowadays. More often than not it is a non-actor. It might be a sportsman (looks good bare-chested) or a 'reality TV personality' or one of those odd modern characters who are known for nothing but being known – the 'celebrity'. They pull the punters, put bums on seats and any lack of acting ability doesn't spoil the show.

It wasn't always thus, of course, but times change and pantos change with them. If the producers think that they'll get additional audience numbers in this way, then they'll do it. If they've miscalculated, it'll be reflected in the box office and they won't do it again, but they've been doing it for some years now, so, no matter what purists may think, they'll carry on doing it until some new fad comes along.

Right: Vicki Michelle as the Wicked Queen in *Snow White* – a part she has played three times: at the Alexandra, Birmingham, in 1998–9; at the Arena, St Albans, in 2000–1; and at the Broadway, Lewisham, in 2001–2.

THE SIDEKICK

Further comic possibilities open up by one or more of the characters having a sidekick, a companion of some sort. The best known – as always – is in *Cinderella*.

Dandini, the Prince's valet, has a long history. First introduced in Rossini's opera, he slipped easily into pantomime versions of the story because there was a Harlequinade character who resembled him, if only in name – the Dandy Lover.

You will remember that the lovers in the original Commedia were not, as they later became in the Harlequinade, Harlequin and Columbine, but were a pair who were more in love with being in love than with each other (see page 15). They dressed in the fashion of the times and not in any form of traditional costume, as the other characters did. They were frequently the butt of satire, where the company mocked contemporary fashion and attitudes, so when, in the Harlequinade, the focus shifted to Harlequin and Columbine, the Dandy Lover remained but changed. He became Pantaloon's choice of husband for Columbine and was rejected by her for all the reasons which made Pantaloon favour him: he

was rich, fashionable to a ridiculous degree, and a pompous, empty-headed fool.

There is no doubt that the fops of Restoration Comedy influenced the Dandy Lover character and, as time passed, he was used to satirize such notables as Beau Brummell and the Prince Regent. Grimaldi had great success in the part and, for a time, the Dandy Lover *was* the Clown.

It would be wrong to say that the Dandini of *La Cenerentola* and the Dandy Lover merged to form the Dandini of *Cinderella*, although it was under that name that Grimaldi played the Dandy Lover. As the comic spotlight swung towards Buttons, Dandini was played down but never entirely lost and he gradually turned into the character we know today. At times he has been played as a second Principal Boy, but the comic potential of the character (particularly in the scene where he swaps clothes and status with the Prince) ensured that more often than not he has remained one of the Comics.

The other character to acquire a sidekick is the baddie. It has become a regular thing for the Demon King or other supernatural baddies to have a human attendant who has to do all the dirty work (and gets it wrong, which causes laughter, so that he is then punished, which makes us laugh again). Named appropriately – Vomit, for example, or, more traditionally, Fleshcreep – he will be sent to spy on the Principal Boy but will almost always switch sides because he is really a nice lad underneath and has simply been corrupted by the Demon King, evil sorcerer or whatever. While we greet the baddie with hisses and boos, before we know it, we will be greeting the sidekick with sympathetic 'ahs' and we will be delighted when the baddie is defeated and the sidekick removed from his evil influence.

Left: Dale Meeks as the baddie Mephisto and Neil Armstrong as his sidekick, Vomit, in *Mother Goose* at the Customs House, South Shields.

Opposite: Julian Clary as the Prince's sidekick, Dandini, in *Cinderella* – a part he has virtually 'owned' in recent years.

THE 'SKIN' PART

Many an established panto performer has started his or her career in one of the 'skin' parts, by which we mean an animal role. There's the cow in *Jack and the Beanstalk*, the cat in *Dick Whittington*, the goose in *Mother Goose*, and numerous pantomime horses and camels, which can crop up almost anywhere.

The 'skin' part might appear to be a thankless role to those who are told that this is to be their introduction to pantomime, but in fact they can be scene-stealers. A sensitive pair of performers playing Daisy (the cow in *Jack and the Beanstalk* is almost always Daisy, although it's occasionally called Gertie or Blossom) can tug at the audience's heartstrings and call forth 'ahs' of sympathy with the flutter of

a long-lashed eye or a drooping head. And with a good rapport between cow and Principal Boy, there can even be tears. I've seen little girls sobbing their hearts out when Jack and Daisy say farewell.

It can be hell in there! Playing the back end of a horse, cow or camel must be a somewhat unpleasant experience which can be made much worse if the person playing the front end is, shall we say, lacking in sensitivity. I remember a production in which the cow was played by two chorus boys. In the green room bar after one show we were all entertained by the 'back end' loudly and obscenely describing just what he would do to his 'front-end' partner if he had another curry during the run of the show!

Even the solo 'skin' parts can be difficult. I popped in to watch a rehearsal for *Mother Goose* at a local theatre recently and eventually left after 30 minutes of watching the director and stage manager trying to get the goose's mechanical bits working properly – with the girl who was playing the goose in the costume, of course. On another occasion during rehearsals, the poor lass also found out how a tortoise feels: she fell over and couldn't get up unaided. Apparently this is almost a tradition with this part.

Probably the most rewarding 'skin' part of all is the Cat in *Dick Whittington*. If Daisy the Cow can steal one scene in *Jack and the Beanstalk*, Tommy the Cat can steal the whole play in *Dick Whittington*. And yet, how Dick ever came to have a cat is not at all clear. There is certainly no cat in the true story of Sir Richard Whittington. Numerous suggestions have been made as to where the cat

Left: One of the great 'skin' parts: the Cat in *Dick Whittington*, here played by 'Mr Albert Felino' in 1908.

Opposite: Barbara Windsor as Jack and Daisy the Cow in *Jack and the Beanstalk* at the Theatre Royal, Newcastle.

we have is the record that it was licensed. However, there is no record of the very respectable Sir Richard ever consorting with such women. The *Cambridge Biographical Encyclopedia* merely states that Whittington's cat is an accepted part of English folklore. The story of him selling the cat to the King of Morocco is similar to a number of tales from around the world, including one from Portugal.

Be this as it may, there is no doubt that Whittington's Cat is the best 'skin' part in the currently popular pantos, only rivalled by Puss in *Puss in Boots*, which is one of the those pantomimes that has fallen out of favour in the last 50 years or so.

There is one 'skin' part that can, and often does, appear in every panto – the Gorilla. He only appears in one scene, behind the Dame, the Clown and any other characters the writer/director/producer cares to put onto the stage, and picks them off one by one. It's the scene, of course, that provides the title for this book – *It's Behind You!* – shouted by the audience to warn the characters, who never think to turn round, of course. No, they walk in a circle, giving the Gorilla the chance to follow them without being seen. Even the smallest kids in the audience are more sensible than them, which is why the kids love panto so much.

role came from in the story. For example, a 'cat' was the nickname of the coal barges that brought Whittington his fortune (although the actual name was the French term *achat*, meaning bargain). The truth is, no one knows. A diligent search for an alternative meaning for 'cat' in the time of the real Whittington (c. 1358–1423) comes up blank. From the sixteenth century to the eighteenth century the term meant prostitute, which is interesting because the earliest record of a play about Whittington with a cat is from 1605, *The History of Richard Whittington, of his Lowe Byrth, his Great Fortune*. The play is now lost and all

Nowadays there aren't any 'skin-part' specialists, but there used to be: Arthur Conquest (1837–1901), Charles Lauri (dates unknown, but appeared throughout the 1890s) and the Griffiths Brothers: Frederick George (1856–1940) and Joe (1853–1901), were all highly esteemed for their performances as a wide range of animals, including kangaroos and donkeys. In the nineteenth century, as now, often the 'skin' parts were given to the newcomers, such as Henry Irving who, at the age of 19, played the leader of a pack of wolves in *Little Bo-Peep* at the Theatre Royal Edinburgh.

THE CHORUS AND BABES

If a modern-day pantomime doesn't kick off with the two major Immortals confronting each other in front of the house tabs (stage curtains) or in front of a decorated gauze, the first scene will be a chorus number.

The chorus has a long history in theatre. In fact, there is one theory, disputed nowadays, that Western theatre began (in Greece) as a choral ode or hymn and at some point a soloist emerged to engage in dialogue with the chorus – the first actor. We see remnants of the chorus in Shakespeare's *Henry V*, and the idea has been revived from time to time by modern dramatists; however, this is a very different beast from the chorus in musical theatre, including opera and pantomime. At its height in classical Greek tragedy, the chorus reflected and commented upon the action, drawing lessons from what the main characters did. Nowadays, the musical theatre chorus is simply the crowd.

In the pantomime the chorus represents the locals, such as the people of Peking in *Aladdin* or

of the local village in most other stories. In the late nineteenth century they really were a crowd, with sometimes hundreds onstage, dressed in extravagant and expensive costumes, but nowadays six girls and four boys would be a large chorus. Economics again. They will be chosen for their looks, and their singing and dancing abilities, not for their acting as their principal job is to sing and dance. One or two may be put into an animal costume to play the 'skin' part (see page 94); all may take part in the schoolroom scene, if the Dame decides to use it. This scene is one of those traditional ones that most often has nothing to do with the plot and is full of dreadful jokes. In it, the

Below: The Babes and the chorus boys strutting their stuff in *Humpty Dumpty* at the Sunderland Empire.

Above: The adorable Babes in rehearsal for a 1970s Newcastle production of *Babes in the Wood*.

new boy (the Comic) invariably introduces himself as Hammond. 'Hammond who?' the Dame asks. 'Ham and eggs,' is the reply. Cue groans from the audience. Chorus members may have a line or two here, but they are most likely to be used as extras.

One of the chorus members will certainly have a line in the opening scene: 'Be careful, Aladdin. The Emperor's daughter is coming through the streets and it is death for anyone who looks upon her.' This kind of fill-in-the-background or move-the-plot-forward line may occur at other points in the show and be given to a member of the chorus, but otherwise they normally don't speak at all.

Chorus members aren't always cast in roles as villagers: sometimes the girls may become fairies, the boys may be footmen at the palace, or both boys and girls may take part in an appropriate ballet sequence at some stage. However, when we compare today's pantos with the Extravaganzas of the late nineteenth century, we realize that the role of the chorus has shrunk almost to vanishing point and that, if it wasn't for the fact that crowd scenes are needed, they probably wouldn't be there at all.

THE BABES

The Babes are the children in the show, normally taken from a single local dance school and varying in age from the very young to about 15. They swell the ranks of the chorus and appear in most of the same scenes. Often they take on smaller skin parts, such as the birds in *Babes in the Wood*, who cover the children with leaves to keep them warm as they sleep. Like the chorus, they will normally have their own moment onstage when they will perform a dance which showcases their strengths as a troupe.

The use of children in pantomime goes back a long way. We have already mentioned the 1899 Drury Lane production of *Jack and the Beanstalk*, which had a large group of children, dressed as soldiers, marching out of the pocket of the dead giant, and how Grimaldi, not yet three years old, broke his collar bone (and could have been killed) in an accident while playing a monkey at Sadler's Wells (1781).

Today, there are many safeguards in law to protect child performers. For example, there normally has to be at least two troupes, for they are only allowed to perform a limited number of times in a week. The regulations regarding the use of children in professional productions are complex and thorough.

Performances are covered by three Acts of Parliament: The Children and Young Persons Act, 1963; the Children (Performances) Regulations, 1968 (as amended) and the Children (Protection at Work) Regulations, 1998 (as amended). Different but very similar regulations apply to Scotland under the Children and Young Persons (Scotland) Act, 1937, and the Children Protection at Work Regulations (Scotland), 2000.

As we've already seen, sometimes the Babes come from a single dance school. A theatre may have a relationship with this school stretching back over a period of years. Sometimes a theatre may have a youth dance group associated with it, and this group will, each year, provide the Babes. Occasionally, a theatre will audition for Babes, but this is the least popular option for the management, because it means that there will be additional expense in carrying out the auditions, rehearsing the children, providing the legally required chaperones and meeting many other legal

Below: A troupe of fairies for a 1912 production of *Aladdin* struggles to hold the pose while the photograph is taken. This picture was used on postcards to promote the panto.

requirements. Taking them from a school or pre-existing organization has many advantages, not least that they will be rehearsed as part of their normal dancing lessons by the teacher who runs the school and he or she will also arrange chaperones – normally the proud parents.

There is a very good reason for having Babes in the show (apart from filling up the crowd scenes), and that is the 'ah!' factor. This is especially potent when very young dancers are used and is always a crowd-pleaser.

You'll notice that the really young children rarely appear in the walk-down at the end of the show during evening performances: that's because the law requires them to be out of the theatre by a certain time, depending on their age. And you'll never see the same troupe twice running. There are always at least two troupes, often three, for the law will only allow them to work for a limited number of hours per week, so theatres tend to rotate the troupes to ensure the Babes have at least every other night off and never do a matinee and an evening performance on the same day.

Interestingly, these rules do not apply to amateur productions or shows put on by schools, only professional performances.

THE MOST POPULAR PANTOS 3

TELLING THE TALE

Many of the best-loved pantomimes have a fascinating history, some stretching back almost 1,000 years with some coming from many parts of the world. All have somehow made their way to the shores of the UK and been turned into a Christmas entertainment for children and families.

In this part we are going to look at some of the most beloved stories and see how they have become the shows we know and love. We won't be looking at some stories because they're much too recent. *Peter Pan*, for example, is not quite 100 years old, having been first performed in 1904, and it didn't get the pantomime treatment until very recently. In fact the story came out of copyright in 1974, and even as late as 1993 it was still regarded purely as a Christmas play, and an alternative to pantomime.

Snow White is another panto that is popular at the moment. It has a long history as a folk tale in many parts of Europe and was first anthologized by the Brothers Grimm around 1815 and translated into English in 1820. However, we won't be looking at in any depth because, despite its interesting background, almost every production is based not on the original but on the Disney film of 1937. Any deviations from *this* 'original' – especially the costume of Snow White herself – are almost inconceivable and would not be welcomed by panto audiences who like continuity and tradition.

We'll look at five of the most popular stories, *Cinderella*, *Aladdin*, *Jack and the Beanstalk*, *Dick Whittington* and *Sleeping Beauty*, together with one that has fallen out of favour in recent years, *Babes in the Wood*.

Why does a panto story fall from favour? It's impossible to say: it just happens. Whatever happened to *Ali Baba and the Forty Thieves*? I saw it a number of times when I was a child in the late 1940s and 1950s, so why did it vanish? Could it have been the necessity for a larger number of performers than usual? Was it a little too close (but not that close, surely?) to *Aladdin*? Or was the story too complex? And what about *Puss in Boots*? It had a bad start at Covent Garden in the first ever production in 1818 (with Grimaldi playing the fairy), when the first night audience rioted and demanded it be taken off! It survived well into the twentieth century, however, but then faded away. Again, perhaps the story was too complex. Perhaps audiences just didn't go for the idea of the central character being the Cat. Whatever the reason, the panto virtually vanished, along with *The Grand Old Duke of York*, *Humpty Dumpty* and many others. Let's take a look at the modern-day survivors, then. They may give us some clue as to what gives a panto longevity.

LYCEUM PANTOMIME

40 THIEVES

PRODUCED BY WALTER and FREDK. MELVILLE

TWICE DAILY at 2 and 7.30

Book of Words :: Price Threepence

Page 52: Bill Owen, Bonnie Langford and Kathy Staff in *Cinderella* in 1984–5. During this press call Bonnie Langford was bitten by a pony and had to have a tetanus jab.

Above: Programme cover for a 1936 production of *40 Thieves*.

CINDERELLA

**Star of ballet, film, musical, novel, opera, pantomime and play.
Of all the pantomime stories, hers is the most widely known.
There are versions of her story from all over the world.**

Ask most people where the story originated and you'll hear mention of Charles Perrault's *Contes de ma Mere L'Oye* (*Tales of Mother Goose*) of 1697, or the early nineteenth-century version found in the Brothers Grimm, where Cinderella is called *Aschenputtel*, the Little Ash Girl. An altogether more grim version than Perrault's, this has the stepsisters having their eyes pecked out by birds at the end, in just recompense for their treatment of *Aschenputtel*. Less well-known is the version by Madame d'Aulnoy (Marie-Cathérine Le Jumel de Barneville de la Motte, Comtesse d'Aulnoy, to give her her full title), published in England in 1721, entitled *The Story of Finetta the Cinder-Girl*. Quite where she got the name Finetta from is not clear, but it was to reappear in the 1820 production at Covent Garden where it was given to the Fairy Godmother.

However, the story of Cinderella is far older than either of these. In fact, the very first Cinderella was Yeh-shen, heroine of a tale first written down by Tuan Ch'eng-shih in ninth-century China. This version has a magic fish instead of a fairy godmother but it does have a gold shoe (not a glass slipper, which many think was a mistake by Perrault confusing *vair*, meaning 'fur', with *verre*, meaning 'glass'). There are also versions from Scotland (*Rashin-Coatie* – in which, with typical Calvinistic piety, Rashin meets the Prince at the kirk or church), from Georgia (*Conkiajgharuna, the Little Rag Girl*) and even Vietnam (*The Story of Tam and Cam*), as well as almost very country in Europe, South America, India and, indeed, almost everywhere

Below: Alex Bogonzi and Alan Rebbeck as the Ugly Sisters in *Cinderella*, in 1989.

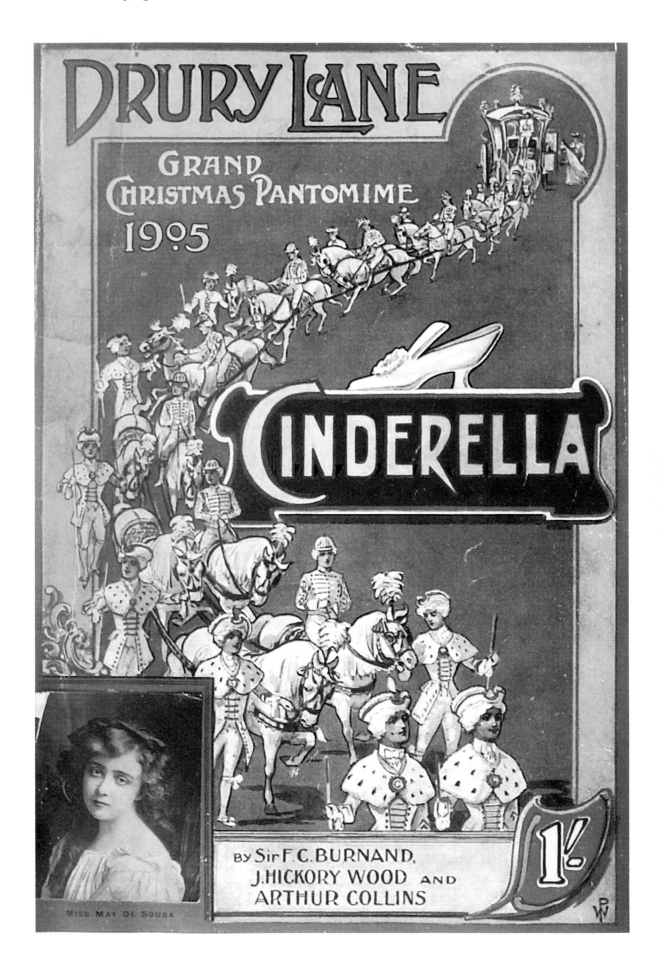

Opposite: Programme cover from one of the pantos by the highly successful team of Burnand, Wood and Collins at the Theatre Royal Drury Lane.

Above: Ian Adams and Jack Wild as the Ugly Sisters in *Cinderella* in a typically happy mood!

else in the world. It is said that there are around 500 versions of the story in Europe alone.

Cinderella the pantomime made its first appearance at Drury Lane in 1804 and appeared again at the Lyceum five years later, but neither was much like the pantomime we know today and certainly did not have many of the characters that we now accept as integral parts of the story. Significantly – for the Cinderella story has had almost as much importance in ballet as in panto – the 1804 production included a *ballet divertissement* of Loves and Graces introduced by the goddess Venus.

In 1817 Gioacchino Rossini's opera *La Cenerentola* (The Ash Girl) opened in the Teatro Valle, Rome. The first night was a disaster and it wasn't until the fifth performance that audiences began to recognize its merit. It moved on to La Scala, Milan, in August of that year and was a resounding success. Encouraged by this, it toured and played in London early in 1820. Twelve weeks later the pantomime *Harlequin and Cinderella; or, the Little Glass Slipper*

was produced at Covent Garden and it was clear that Rossini's opera had had an effect. In the panto, Cinderella's father became a baron (he was first given that rank by Rossini) and Dandini and the cruel (but not ugly) stepsisters appeared (again, first seen in Rossini). This was also the first version to feature a Dame – the Baroness, played by Grimaldi.

Just two years later, London's King's Theatre presented the ballet *Cendrillon* (the French name for Cinderella), which also followed the Rossini opera very closely. It transferred to Paris the following year and remained in the repertoire there until 1831, receiving 111 performances in that time.

It was not until 1860, however, that the modern *Cinderella* pantomime emerged. This was *Cinderella; or, The Lover, the Lackey, and the Little Glass Slipper*, a 'fairy burlesque extravaganza' by H. J. Byron at the Strand Theatre. Here Buttons (as Buttoni) makes his first appearance and the unkind, even nasty, sisters become ugly. It only required the arrival of the Broker's Men to complete the modern cast. They arrived, not in London but in my own home town of Sunderland where, in 1880, they appeared for the first time as a 'Chorus of Broker's Men'. By 1883 they had made their way to London and reached the Drury Lane stage – a sure sign of acceptance – in 1895.

The ballet *Cendrillon* moved to Moscow in 1825, where it opened the new Bolshoi Petrovsky Theatre.

BALLET OF
THE UGLY SISTERS
(see inside)

PICTURE POST

36 PAGES

Discovery that Opens Africa:
DRUG MEANS MORE FOOD

Vol. 42. No. 3

JANUARY 15, 1949

4D

professional productions in England alone and it has remained the most popular pantomime until very recently, when it has begun to be overtaken by *Aladdin*. Every pantomime writer produces a version of *Cinderella*; Rodgers and Hammerstein made a musical based on the story, originally for CBS television, which was staged at the London Coliseum in 1958; Disney produced a cartoon version; Mary Pickford appeared in a 1914 film version; Eleanor Farjeon wrote a novel on the theme *The Glass Slipper*; there was another musical film version in 1976 (*The Slipper and the Rose*, directed by Bryan Forbes); and, of course, between 1940 and 1944 Prokofiev wrote a version for the Kirov Ballet, which was originally choreographed by Rostislav Zakharov, and, more memorably, in 1948 by Frederick Ashton. The role of Cinderella in Ashton's ballet was created by Moira Shearer because Margot Fonteyn was injured, and Ashton and Robert Helpmann played the Ugly Sisters.

Cinderella is the only panto ever to be produced by the National Theatre, opening at the Lyttelton on 15 December 1983. Directed by Bill Bryden with set design by William Dudley, it starred Janet Dibley as Cinderella, Marsha Hunt as Dandini, Tony Haygarth as Buttons and Susan Fleetwood as the Fairy Godmother. Sadly it wasn't a success.

Why does this simple story hold such fascination? Well, one Beryl Sanford, writing in *The Psychoanalytical Forum* in 1967 suggests that 'the Ugly Sisters's attempts to fit their feet into the slipper are castration attempts to have female genitalia' and Cinderella rejects Buttons ('the only human being in this galaxy of Panto mortals and immortals') in favour of 'an ideal combined mother-father figure'. I rather think that the appeal lies in the triumph of the underdog over those who not only have power over her, but have abused that power. And as for Buttons, at the end he represents the bittersweetness of self-sacrifice for the happiness of the loved one, the sort of person we would like to think we could be.

Cinderella has now dropped from the number one spot it occupied for more than a century, and has been replaced by the panto we will look at next, *Aladdin*.

A new Moscow version, *Cinderella, or the Golden Slipper*, followed in 1871, created by the Czech choreographer Vaclav Reisinger, and in 1893 another version opened in St Petersburg, created by Marius Petipa, Enrico Cecchetti and Lev Ivanov.

The worlds of ballet and pantomime are not as far apart as you might imagine, and in 1883–84 one of Britain's leading dancers, Kate Vaughan, was cast as Cinderella, to great acclaim.

There were more than 90 productions of *Cinderella* during the nineteenth century. The story was the most commonly used in France for dance pieces and, in 1899, Georges Méliès made the first film version of the story, one that broke many early cinema traditions and introduced techniques which are still part of movie-making today (such as shooting a number of different scenes instead of just one, and then linking them together using dissolves).

As we move into the twentieth century, it is clear that the Cinderella story continues to fascinate audiences. In 1948, for example, there were 37 different

★ THE STORY OF CINDERELLA ★

Cinderella is the daughter of Baron Hardup. Her mother dies and her father marries again but his new wife proves to be a thoroughly nasty person – the archetypal wicked stepmother. She already has two daughters who are totally spoilt – the Ugly Sisters. In most modern pantos the stepmother no longer appears, as three Dames would be just too much, whereas having two works well.

The Uglies (their popular stage name) treat Cinderella as a slave, forcing her to work as a scullery maid and to look after them. Although she is her father's favourite, he is too weak to stand up to the Uglies. Cinders, however, has one friend, the page Buttons, who is very much in love with her. She confides in him and he tries to keep her cheerful.

One day the King announces that he is to hold a ball in honour of his son, Prince Charming, and invites all the nobility and gentry. An invitation, of course, comes to Baron Hardup's castle but the Uglies refuse to countenance the idea of Cinders attending. Instead she is forced to wash and iron their ball gowns and help them with their preparations. Finally they go off to the ball and Cinders is left, sitting miserably among the ashes in the kitchen.

Suddenly a magical woman appears, her Fairy Godmother, who tells her that she will go to the ball. Using her magic wand, the Fairy Godmother brings about the transformation scene in which Cinders's rags turn into a sumptuous ball gown, her battered old shoes to glass slippers, a pumpkin turns into a coach and mice become horses. Off she goes to the ball, with a warning from the Fairy Godmother that she must return by midnight, when all the magic will be undone.

At the ball everyone wonders who this mysterious great beauty is and Prince Charming falls for her in a big way. They dance together all evening until suddenly she realizes it is almost midnight and flees from the palace, accidentally leaving behind one of her glass slippers.

The Prince scours the kingdom for his mysterious love, announcing that he will marry the girl whose foot the glass slipper will fit. No foot fits it, however, and eventually, at the end of his quest, he arrives at Castle Hardup. The Uglies try all means to squeeze their big feet into the slipper.

Cue one of the oldest jokes in panto. Sister One says, 'I can't get my foot into the crystal slipper.' Sister Two replies, 'You couldn't get your foot into the Crystal Palace!'

However, they fail and the Prince is devastated, for this is his last port of call. Someone – in some versions it is Buttons, in others it's the Baron – mentions Cinderella, and the Uglies, of course, forbid her to try on the slipper. The Prince, however, insists. Cinders tries it on and, of course, the slipper fits perfectly. They marry and, in the best pantomime tradition, live happily ever after.

ALADDIN

Let's be correct: this pantomime's proper name is *Aladdin and his Wonderful Lamp*,
although you'll rarely find it getting its full title nowadays. The story comes from
the *Thousand and One Nights* (also called the *Arabian Nights Entertainment*),
which is the collection of tales told by Scheherazade, tales which come from
a variety of sources but are thought to have been first collected together
in Persia (now Iran) in the ninth century.

A papyrus mentions a *Book of Stories from the Thousand Nights*. In the tenth century there is mention by one contemporary historian of translations made in Baghdad of stories from Persian, Indian and Greek sources, among which was a book called *A Thousand Tales* (*Alf khurâfah*), also known as *A Thousand Nights* (*Alf laylah*). The source of the version we know is a fifteenth-century Egyptian manuscript, which gave rise to a Syrian text that was translated into French by Antoine Galland.

Galland had bought a copy of the book when he was serving as assistant to the French Ambassador in Istanbul in the first two decades of the eighteenth century. The first story (or rather, stories, for there were eight of them: an introduction, followed by seven actual tales) to appear in English was that of Sinbad the Sailor, a version of which was published in 1712. The story of Aladdin (or, more properly, 'Ala-ed-Din) was published about ten years later, at the same time as the story of Ali Baba and the Forty

Opposite: Comedian Steve Barclay makes an entrance as Widow Twankey in *Aladdin* in 2001.

Above: *Aladdin* handbill from a Theatre Royal production c. 1930.

Thieves. However, it was more than 60 years later, in 1788, that the story was first used in a pantomime at Covent Garden. The costumes, we are told, were inspired by a variety of national dress – Chinese, Japanese and Persian – and that was to become the norm. Even today, the names of the characters, their costumes and even the settings are a strange mixture of Arab and Chinese.

Aladdin's real name ('Ala-ed-Din) in the *Thousand and One Nights* is Arabic. His father was Mustapha, a poor tailor, and it was the daughter of the sultan with whom he fell in love. Somehow, by the time the story became established as a panto, the location has switched from Baghdad to Peking and his mother has become a washerwoman who runs the local (later still, the imperial) laundry. She has become

Widow Twankey, the sultan has become the Emperor of China and his daughter the Lady Badroubaldor. We see the change beginning to happen in 1813, when Charles Farley produced another version (not a pantomime) at Covent Garden, renaming Aladdin's mother Ching Mustapha. In the nineteenth century people were fascinated by all things oriental, and *chinoiserie* was particularly popular: this is almost certainly what lies behind the eastward shift of the story.

Like *Cinderella*, the story of Aladdin went through a process of development until it achieved stability. Yet again, it was the influence of H. J. Byron which was decisive. His Extravaganza *Aladdin; or the Wonderful Scamp* was presented at the Strand Theatre in 1861 and was the very first to name

ALADDIN

DAN CRAWLEY & HARRY LAUDER
(THE TEA ROOM SCENE)

Above: Handbill for a 1905 production starring the hugely popular coalminer-turned-comedian Harry Lauder.

Opposite: *Aladdin* at the Empire Theatre, Sunderland, in 1976.

Aladdin's mother Widow Twankey. This was the precursor to all modern productions, although Byron was not responsible for the introduction of Wishee

Washee – that honour goes to the Drury Lane production of 1896.

Aladdin was also 'responsible' for a major shift in tradition in the twentieth century. As we looked at on page 59, the 1956–57 season at the London Palladium dispensed with a female Principal Boy in its production, casting Norman Wisdom as Aladdin – an idea which was taken up by many other theatres. It is true that they reverted back to female Principal Boys in 1971, but since then producers have felt free to cast men or women in the part, and it is probably true to say that today there are as many productions with a man in the lead role as there are traditional ones.

In spite of its long history, *Aladdin* has not inspired the huge number of adaptations that *Cinderella* has. There have been 41 films based on the story (compared to 94 for *Cinderella*), the most successful being Disney's 1992 full-length animation. Others have come from Mexico, India, the former Soviet Union, Italy, Turkey and Germany. Strangely enough, none have come from China or Hong Kong (though the latter did produce two versions of *Cinderella*). Although there have been ballets on the subject, very few have entered the established repertoire and only one was created before the second half of the twentieth century (1843, choreographed by August Bournonville).

In recent years, *Aladdin* has always been one of the top two pantos as far as the number of major professional productions is concerned. It had always taken second place to *Cinderella* until 2003, when it overtook poor Cinders in frequency of production.

Will *Aladdin* stay there, with *Snow White*, who has pushed Cinders down into third place? It's hard to say, but one thing we can be sure of: Aladdin is going to be rubbing his magic lamp and courting the princess for some time to come!

☆ THE STORY OF ALADDIN ☆

One day Aladdin hears that the Emperor of China's daughter will be walking through the city and he decides to hide and take a look at her, even though it means death for anyone caught doing so. He sees her and falls in love. (In some versions of the tale he meets her unwittingly and they fall in love with each other, and in some versions he doesn't see her at all until later in the pantomime.)

The family is visited by the magician Abanazar, who is usually described as being from Africa, most often Morocco or Egypt. Abanazar claims to be Aladdin's long-lost uncle. He asks Aladdin to do him a favour. When Aladdin agrees, Abanazar takes him to a cave, which he opens with a magic spell, and asks Aladdin to go in and fetch him a magic lamp, which is said to be in the cave. Aladdin is afraid, so Abanazar gives him a ring, which, he says, will protect Aladdin from harm.

Aladdin goes into the cave and finds the lamp but refuses to hand it over until he is out of the cave. Abanazar demands it immediately, but Aladdin continues to refuse. In a rage, Abanazar casts another spell, locking Aladdin in the cave.

In misery, Aladdin rubs his hands together, thereby rubbing the ring, and a genie (a *djinn* in Arabic) appears, offering to grant him a wish. Aladdin wishes to be released from the cave and be taken home, and this is what happens. The lamp, of course, goes with him.

Later Aladdin (or his mother) attempts to clean the lamp, which is rather dirty, and an even more powerful genie appears. The genie tells Aladdin that he will grant him anything he desires: 'Your wish is my command, oh master!' Aladdin wishes for great wealth, which is, of course, provided.

As a wealthy man, Aladdin now approaches the Emperor and asks for his daughter's hand in marriage. The Emperor, unwilling that she should marry a commoner, says that Aladdin may only wed her if he builds a rich palace for her overnight. This is no problem to the genie, and so Aladdin and the Princess (traditionally called Badroubaldor, although more often nowadays Jasmine, following the Disney cartoon) become engaged – or even, in some versions, married.

Abanazar, however, has not given up hope of obtaining the magic lamp and so, disguised as a wandering merchant, passes through the streets of Peking offering 'new lamps for old'. The Princess, not knowing the lamp's powers, takes him up on the offer and Abanazar is triumphant. Here the stories diverge.

In the original (and usual) version, Abanazar has Aladdin and his family transported magically to the deserts of Africa, and Aladdin uses the powers of the Genie of the Ring to transport them back to China on a magic carpet. Aladdin then seeks out Abanazar, defeats him, regains the lamp and his wealth, marries the Princess and lives happily ever after.

In the alternative version, Aladdin sets off on a quest to find Abanazar and regain the ring. This takes him to Africa, where he finds and defeats him. Our hero then returns to Peking to marry the Princess and, of course, live happily ever after.

JACK AND THE BEANSTALK

Since David the Israelite brought down Goliath of Gath with a pebble, there have been stories of boys who confront and defeat giants. It's a common enough story in the folk tales of many countries, mainly in northern and central Europe, particularly Finland and Norway, but there are also versions in Romania and Spain. Stories of giants being defeated by superhero boys began to spread in this country about the same time as the Saxon invasion (sixth century) and the most well known, prior to the first-known appearance of *Jack and the Beanstalk* in the early eighteenth century, was the old Cornish legend of *Jack the Giant Killer*.

The Cornish legend is at least 1,000 years old. Certainly, the idea that Cornwall and, in fact, the whole of Britain was the home of giants was known to Geoffrey of Monmouth because he states in his *History of the Kings of Britain* (c. 1135–36) that Brutus, the grandson of Aeneas, travelled to Britain with his deputy Corineus who defeated the king of the giants Gogmagog in a wrestling match. Corineus then settled down in the area, which was named after him and is now known as Cornwall. Brutus then went on to conquer the rest of the country, clearing it of giants.

I hasten to point out, of course, that Geoffrey is not regarded as a reliable historical source, although he is reliable in retelling the legends of his time.

In any case, the story of *Jack the Giant Killer* is linked with the legend of King Arthur, for it was to him

that Jack took the head of Cormoran, the first giant he slew. After that he went on to kill many more, including the giant Blunderbore, the name which is traditionally given to the giant in *Jack and the Beanstalk*. Could it be that one story is just a version of the other? This has certainly been suggested, but, while we have written evidence of the more basic *Jack the Giant Killer* story from a fairly early time, the Jack and the beanstalk story first appears in written form in a 1734 reprint of a book first published in 1730, *Round About our Coal-Fire: or Christmas Entertainments*. This contained a parody of the story, entitled *Enchantment demonstrated in the Story of Jack Spriggins and the Enchanted Bean*. It is also interesting that, although the first stage version of *Jack the Giant Killer* was presented by Garrick as a Christmas play in 1733, it was not until 1819 that *Jack and the Beanstalk* made its first appearance, as a pantomime at Drury Lane under the title *Jack and the Beanstalk; or, Harlequin and the Ogre*. This was probably the very first panto to have a female Principal Boy (Eliza Povey).

Drury Lane produced another imaginative version in 1859, which began high above the ground, and probably the most spectacular ever in 1899. Not only did a crowd of children in British Army uniforms emerge from the dead giant's pockets (thus providing a patriotic note), but it also included a parade of heroines from Shakespeare's plays, who emerged from books in the giant's library. This satisfied the need for the by then mandatory educational pageant.

The opportunity for spectacular effects is one of the story's great attractions to producers, even without the Victorian educational embellishments. Designers have exercised great ingenuity in creating giants which at times have filled the stage, and even greater ingenuity in the choreography of the fierce fight between Blunderbore and Jack. And, going to exactly the opposite extreme, very few producers or directors can resist the temptation of making sure there isn't a dry eye in the house when the cow (usually called Daisy) learns it is to be sold.

Jack the Giant Killer had a few productions in the early nineteenth century, but it was soon outstripped by its younger sibling, which has remained popular to this day. Now *Jack and the Beanstalk* is one of the top five pantos, whereas the other is hardly ever seen.

Opposite: Marc Symour as Dame Trot and Steven Day as Silly Billy in a 2002–3 production of *Jack and the Beanstalk* at the Kenneth More Theatre, in Ilford.

Above: Dolly Castles as Jack and George Graves as Mrs Halleybutt in *Jack and the Beanstalk* at the Theatre Royal Drury Lane, c. 1911.

☆ THE STORY OF JACK AND THE BEANSTALK ☆

Jack, who is usually portrayed as being a lazy young man, and his mother are very poor. They are so poor, indeed, that they are forced to sell their only valuable possession, their cow. Jack is sent to the local village market to find a buyer but, being lazy, when he is accosted by someone who offers him a handful of beans, he accepts rather than walk the extra distance. His mother is predictably furious and throws the beans out of the window. The following morning the beans have grown and a huge beanstalk reaches up to the sky. Jack climbs to the top and finds himself in a giant's castle. There he steals a hen that lays golden eggs.

The following day he climbs again and steals the giant's bag of gold and the next day he tries to steal his golden harp. However, the harp cries out and wakes the giant who chases after Jack. He shins rapidly down the beanstalk, grabs an axe and chops it down. The giants falls from the sky and is killed. This, of course, is just the basic story and pantomime writers have added all kinds of extra characters, sub-plots and incidents.

Opposite and above: The props and sets required for *Jack and the Beanstalk* to be performed convincingly are significant.

In the original story, Jack is portrayed as being a wastrel who impoverishes his mother through his spendthrift lifestyle. Pantomime, as it does, has sentimentalized the story and he becomes lazy but good-hearted. And of course new characters have been added: a heroine; the giant's sidekick (named Fleshcreep by modern panto writer John Morley); a fairy (Morley also invented the Vegetable Fairy!); various parts for comics; and, such is the nature of the modern pantomime, almost anything that the writer wants to add! For example, many writers have added a Mrs Giant and sometimes the Giant has been the proud possessor of the goose that lays golden eggs. He has also, at times, had a singing harp which would sound to warn him if anyone other than himself touched it. Sometimes the Giant is killed when he chases Jack down the beanstalk and Jack cuts it down. In other versions, the Giant and Jack fight in the Giant's castle in the sky, and Jack defeats him either by superior swordsmanship or trickery.

A number of traditions have grown up around Jack. For example, his mother is almost always known nowadays as Dame Trot, but she was called Dame Durden more frequently in the nineteenth century. And now, of course, there is Daisy the Cow (who has been called Gertie in the past), whose big eyes and fluttering eyelashes create enormous sympathy in the audience when Jack has to sell her.

And of course, what production would be complete without the Giant crying out:

Fee, fi, fo, fum,
I smell the blood of an Englishman!

DICK WHITTINGTON

Dick Whittington is the only popular pantomime that is based on a real person. All the rest come from fairy or folk tales, but Dick Whittington was a real man – and he was Lord Mayor of London not thrice but four times.

Sir Richard Whittington, as he became, was born in Pauntley in Gloucestershire in 1358, the youngest son of Sir William Whittington. His father died when Richard was 13 and so, being the youngest son, he had to find some way of supporting himself if he was not to be dependent upon the 'charity' of his eldest brother, so he went to London where he took up an apprenticeship.

Dick became a merchant in the textile trade – a mercer – specializing in rare and expensive cloths, and married Alice, the daughter of Sir Ivo Fitzwaryn. As a merchant he was extremely successful and became Sheriff in 1393 and then Lord Mayor of London four times: 1397–98, 1398–99, 1406–07 and yet again in 1419–20.

The first term as Lord Mayor came about when the previous incumbent died in office and Whittington

was appointed to the post by Richard II. Whittington was elected the following year at the end of his appointed tenure of the post. He made loans to Henry IV and Henry V, and was also well known for his charitable work. The charity that was set up in 1424 thanks to a bequest Whittington made of £5,000 (a sum equivalent to several millions in today's terms) still exists, with the aim of providing 'Almshouses for almspeople who shall be poor women of good character who are not less than 55 years of age and payments of stipends to such persons; payments of pensions to members of the Mercers' Company and their families who are in need, hardship or distress; relief of persons who are in conditions of need, hardship or distress.' The fund is still administered by the Mercers' Company, one of the major livery companies of the City of London, of which Whittington was Master three times.

In some ways, *Dick Whittington* the panto is like *Cinderella* – a kind of rags to riches story, except that in real life it is highly unlikely that Whittington ever experienced the 'rags' side of things. Although he was a younger son and the main part of the family wealth and property went, on his father's death, to his oldest brother, Dick would have been reasonably provided for, and learning the mercer's trade would have ensured a comfortable independence (or rather more than that, in his case). However, he was certainly an outsider, coming to London, marrying a rich man's daughter and going on to achieve high office. But, as far as we know, the real Dick Whittington didn't lose a cat.

Outside of historical documents, the first mention of Whittington in a literary work is a now lost play entitled *The History of Richard Whittington, of his Lowe Byrth, his Great Fortune*. By the time of this play (it was licensed in 1605), we see that his story

Left: An imaginary portrait of Dick Whittington surrounded by scenes from his life, by John Glover.

Opposite: Sybil Arundale (and an unidentified poor soul in the 'skin' part) in *Dick Whittington*.

★ THE STORY OF DICK WHITTINGTON ★

Dick is the son of poor parents. On hearing that the streets of London are paved with gold, he sets off there to make his fortune. He meets and befriends a cat, then obtains menial work with Alderman Fitzwarren and falls in love with Fitwarren's daughter, Alice. However, he is falsely accused of a crime and is sacked. He decides he will leave London.

On his way out of the city, Dick rests (or, in some versions, falls asleep) on Highgate Hill, where he hears (or dreams he hears) the bells calling out: 'Turn again, Whittington, Lord Mayor of London'. This persuades him not to give up and he returns to the city where he and the cat rid the inhabitants of a great plague of rats.

Whittington then joins one of Alderman Fitzwarren's ships and sails to somewhere exotic (often Morocco), where he again meets, fights and defeats the Rat King and is rewarded with great riches. He returns home, marries Alice, becomes Lord Mayor of London and lives happily ever after.

Like the *Jack and the Beanstalk* story, this one has been expanded by writers, who have added a Fairy of the Bells, a Cook (the Dame), shipwreck and even an underwater scene.

has been changed, and the fact that Whittington's father was a knight of the shire had been forgotten. This play is referred to in Beaumont and Fetcher's *The Knight of the Burning Pestle* (1611). Samuel Pepys mentions in his Diary that in 1668 he saw – and enjoyed, which was something that he didn't often do – a puppet show about Whittington.

It was just over 200 years later, in 1814, that the pantomime version first appeared. This was *Dick Whittington; or, the Lord Mayor of London* at Covent Garden, starring Joseph Grimaldi as Dame Cecily Suet. It became a popular panto thereafter, and two productions in the late nineteenth/early twentieth century were responsible for the popularizing of two very different songs.

In the 1891–92 production at the Grand Theatre, Islington, the Music Hall star Lottie Collins first sang what was to be her theme tune, a song which still survives to this day, 'Ta-ra-ra-boom-de-ay'. Then in 1908–9, at Drury Lane, Wilkie Bard (1870–1944), playing Idle Jack, first sang 'She Sells Sea-Shells on the Sea Shore', one of the best-known tongue-twisters of all time.

Probably the most successful male cast in the role of Principal Boy was pop singer Tommy Steele, who twice appeared as Dick Whittington, once on television (where he wrote a number of the songs) and once at the London Palladium (1969). In fact, many believe him to have been the best in the part in the twentieth century.

Dick Whittington became the first ever pantomime to be recognized by the educational establishment when John Morley's version was a set text for the National Curriculum in English in 1992. It is a panto worth studying, for not only does it show something

of how a true story can be changed over the years, but it also has one of the classic baddies – King Rat.

Ring a ring of rosies
A pocket full of posies
A-tishoo! A-tishoo!
We all fall down

That sweet little nursery rhyme isn't really sweet at all. It's all about the plague. People tried to protect themselves from the plague by keeping posies of sweet-smelling flowers to their noses to keep out the contagion. But, of course, it didn't work; the symptoms developed and 'we all fall down' dead. The plague was not confined to the outbreaks that are well-known today, but was a constant fear for centuries. The precise means by which the disease was passed on by rats was not understood, but the connection was recognized. So King Rat was more than a figure in a story: he was the personification of a very real and ever-present danger. Witches, bad fairies, cruel stepmothers, all paled into insignificance in the face of the symbol of the worst disease (after leprosy) known to man. Even today, people who have never seen a rat shudder at the thought of them. Fear of rats seems to be ingrained in our collective subconscious.

A rags to riches story, a fearsome villain with both supernatural and natural characteristics, a superb 'skin' part, and the opportunity for spectacular scenes (when, for example, Dick's ship sinks) all add up to a perfect pantomime story, which is why it has remained in the top five for so long.

Right: Keith Hopkins as Sarah the Cook in *Dick Whittington*.

SLEEPING BEAUTY

Like many pantomime tales, *Sleeping Beauty* has a long history. We first hear mention of the tale in the *Thousand and One Nights*, where it is known as the *Ninth Captain's Tale*.

In the *Thousand and One Nights* the heroine we know as Beauty is called Sittukhan. She is the daughter of an ordinary woman who could not conceive, not a king. The woman prays to Allah for a child: 'Give me a daughter, even if she be not proof against the smell of flax!' And so the beautiful Sittukhan is born.

When the child is ten, a prince falls in love with her but, by accident, a piece of flax gets under her fingernail and she falls as if dead. The original story then diverges somewhat from the one we know today, involving falseness on the part of the prince who claims to love her, a magic ring known as the ring of Sulaiman, which (like Aladdin's) is used to build a magnificent palace overnight, and Sittukhan's revenge. But of course Sittukhan and the prince do live happily ever after and, as the story says, 'They dwelt together in love delight.'

The same story, if somewhat changed, reappears in 1634 in Naples in *Il Pentamerone*, a collection of stories by Giambattista Basile, under the title 'Sun, Moon and Talia' (Talia being the name given to the heroine). This 'Beauty' is the much-loved daughter of a lord and, like Sittukhan, her weakness is flax: coming into contact with it would kill her. Again, like Sittukhan, some flax gets underneath her nail and she falls dead on the ground. Her grieving father places her in a chair in the castle's salon and abandons her in grief.

Thereafter the tale becomes blacker: Talia is raped by a passing king, gives birth to twins and is finally awakened when a fairy places them at her breast. However, they cannot find her nipples so they suck on her fingers instead, and out comes the flax. Talia is revived. But the happy ending doesn't come yet: the children (called Sun and Moon) are carried off by the jealous queen who tells the palace cook to kill them and serve them to her husband in a pie. He doesn't, of course, but he takes the children home and he and his wife bring them up as their own. Eventually everything ends happily: the wicked queen is burned to death, the children are restored to their mother, the king marries Talia and the cook becomes chamberlain.

It is likely that Basile took the story from a fourteenth-century French romance called *Perceforest*, which has a very similar plot, in which the heroine, here named Zellandine, is also raped by a passing king. The story reappears in Perrault's *Mother Goose Tales* in 1696 with some differences. The beginning is as we know it but Perrault keeps the wicked queen, whom he says is an ogress, and the attempted cannibalism.

Opposite: Three good fairies! Jean Southern, Helen Russell and Gwen Doran had such a great hit in the comedy *Dirty Dusting* at the Customs House, South Shields, that they were all invited back to play the good fairies in *Sleeping Beauty* in 2003.

Right: Handbill for a 1932 production at the Lyceum, starring Kitty Reidy, Naughton & Gold, and Dick Tubb.

LYCEUM PANTOMIME

SLEEPING BEAUTY

PRODUCED BY WALTER & FREDK. MELVILLE

TWICE DAILY at 2 and 7.30

It is not until 1812 that we find the version we know today in *Little Briar-Rose* by the Brothers Grimm. The first British dramatization of the story was a melodrama *The Sleeping Beauty, a Grand Legendary Melodrama* at Drury Lane in 1806. It was not until 1822 that it was first performed as a pantomime, *Harlequin and the Ogress; or, the Sleeping Beauty of the Wood* , by Charles Farley at Covent Garden. This starred Grimaldi who was, by this time, very close to the end of his career. Planché presented it as an Extravaganza at Covent Garden in 1840, and Dan Leno (as Queen Ravia) and Herbert Campbell (King Screwdolph) starred in a Drury Lane version by J. Hickory Wood in 1900.

Much more recently, in 1967, Danny La Rue made his mark in panto in *Queen Passionella and the Sleeping Beauty* at the Saville Theatre, which holds the record for being London's longest-running

Above: The Prince about to wake the Sleeping Beauty with a kiss, from a 2002 production at the Kenneth More Theatre, Ilford, starring Lee Bright and Clare Cunliffe.

Opposite: De Hally as Loyse and Jean Perier as Olivier, in a production of *Sleeping Beauty*. This photograph appeared in *Le Theatre* in April 1900.

pantomime ever. Whether this has more to do with La Rue or the story of *Sleeping Beauty* is, of course, a point for debate. The story did, however, prove an appropriate subject for a ballet, which, written by Tchaikovsky in 1890, has become a regular part of the international ballet repertoire.

Disney produced a cartoon version of the story in 1958 in which, incidentally, the figure of Princess Aurora (the Sleeping Beauty) was modelled on Audrey Hepburn.

★ THE STORY OF SLEEPING BEAUTY ★

Late in their lives a king and queen have a child for whom they have longed for many, many years. Sometimes the child is named Beauty, sometimes Rose, and sometimes some other name. In a great celebration, they invite everyone who is anyone, including all the fairies in the land, to a fabulous party at the palace. However, they forget (or deliberately omit) to invite Carabosse, a wicked fairy (in some versions, a witch), who nonetheless comes and, in revenge for being slighted, puts a curse on the child. The curse says the child will prick her finger and die. A good fairy defends our heroine, however, by changing the outcome of the curse from death to 100 years of sleep.

Naturally, Beauty's parents do all they can to make sure that this can never happen, and everything which can possibly prick her finger is banished from the castle. Even the roses in the gardens have their thorns removed.

All goes well for 15 or 16 years until one day the princess, wandering in a disused part of the castle, comes across an old woman using a spinning wheel. In most versions, the old woman is, in fact, Carabosse, determined that her curse will come true. Fascinated by what the old woman

is doing, for she has not seen a spinning wheel before, the princess picks up the spindle, pricks her finger, and instantly everyone in the castle falls into a deep sleep. A great hedge grows around the castle, cobwebs cover everything (including the characters), and it and its inhabitants are forgotten.

One day, 100 years later, a prince comes riding by, forces his way through the hedge and into the castle, finds the sleeping princess and is so overcome by her beauty that he leans down and kisses her. She immediately wakes, as does everyone else in the castle. She sees the prince, falls in love, they marry and live happily ever after.

As with all the other pantomime stories, *Sleeping Beauty* has been embellished by writers over the years and all the traditional panto elements, such as a Dame and a comic, for example, have been added.

BABES IN THE WOOD

The pantomime *Babes in the Wood* links together two English legends: the story of
two children abandoned to die in a wood by a wicked uncle
and the world-renowned figure of Robin Hood.

The ballad *The Children in the Wood; or, the Norfolk Gentleman's Last Will and Testament*, was recorded as having been printed at Stationers' Hall in 1595, and is almost certainly based on an older traditional story. There is a version from the Southern Appalachian mountains in the USA and it can be traced back to yet another version mentioned in a collection called *Percy's Reliques* (1601), which attributed it to one Robert Tarrington.

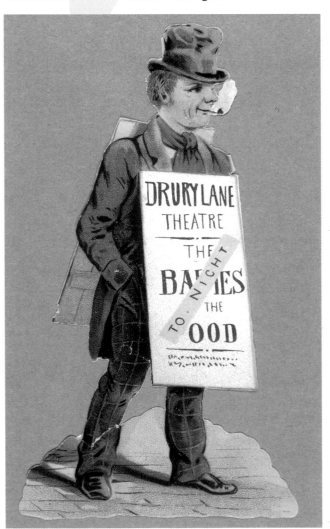

The theme of abandoning children goes back to the ancient Greeks. Oedipus was 'exposed' and left on Mount Cithaeron to die, because of a prophecy which said that he would kill his father and marry his mother. He would certainly have died were it not for the fact that the shepherd who was supposed to abandon him felt guilty and passed him to another shepherd from the neighbouring country. In fact, this kind of exposure was not uncommon for unwanted children, especially girls. The reason for 'exposing' these children was that, by leaving them to die rather than actually killing them, the perpetrators would avoid the attention of the Furies whose job it was to avenge the spilling of kindred blood.

The story of the English legend is that the two children were orphaned and left a huge fortune, which was held in trust for them by their uncle. The uncle, determined to get his hands on their money, pays two ruffians to take them into the woods and murder them. One, however, takes pity on them and kills his companion, then flees. The children eventually die and a robin covers their bodies with leaves. Later bad luck stalks the uncle and he loses everything, finally dying in prison. The ruffian who had saved them was condemned to death as a highway robber.

The first stage version of the story was an opera, performed at the Theatre Royal Haymarket in 1793, *The Children in the Wood*. It first appeared as a pantomime in 1827 at Drury Lane under the title *Harlequin and Cock Robin; or, the Babes in the Wood*. It kept the tragic ending, as did further productions at the Haymarket (1856) and Covent Garden (1874), although the latter did have the

Left: Illustration of a sandwichman advertising a *Babes in the Wood* production at Drury Lane, in the late nineteenth century.

Opposite: Illustration from *The Christmas Pantomime* children's book, c. 1890. In modern pantos the children are always played by a girl and a boy.

Left: The heat of battle in a 1999–2000 production of *Robin Hood*.

Below: Proud chorus girls from a 1970s production of *Babes in the Wood*.

wicked uncle coming to a bad end. The 'Cock Robin' reference refers to the bodies of the children being covered by a robin, for there is an old wives' tale that robins will not leave bodies of any kind unburied.

In 1867 the character of Robin Hood was introduced. He saves the children and helps them unmask their wicked uncle, which is the storyline that is followed to this day. The robin, by the way, remains, except that he is usually joined by others and they cover the children with leaves to protect them from the elements when they fall asleep. Because the original old wives' tale has passed out of use, these days instead of robins there is a variety of small forest animals played by the Babes, the juvenile dancers.

Robin Hood is one of the archetypal folk heroes and his story has given rise to countless versions in all sorts of media, particularly film (including the classic Errol Flynn version) and television. The story's classic ingredients – an aristocrat driven from his inheritance for his loyalty to an absent king, an evil adversary in the Sheriff of Nottingham, a love affair, robbing from the rich to give to the poor, his timely rescue by the return of the king – have ensured that Robin Hood has held the imagination of audiences for centuries and it would have been surprising if he had not appeared in a pantomime.

The earliest version of the Robin Hood story, *A Gest of Robyn Hode*, probably dates from 1450 or even earlier. Already here we find that the outlaw will not rob the poor or the good, just the rich and evil:

★ THE STORY OF BABES IN THE WOOD ★

Two children, a boy and a girl whose names vary from panto to panto, are left in the care of their uncle on the death of their father. The uncle, eager to get his hands on the fortune left in trust for the children, arranges for them to be taken into the forest and murdered. One of the murderers, however, stricken by conscience, kills his partner and runs off, leaving the children to fend for themselves.

The babes wander alone, staying alive by eating blackberries. When they collapse, exhausted, at the end of the day, they are covered with leaves by birds (or, sometimes, by small forest animals such as rabbits) to keep them warm. The children are eventually rescued by Robin Hood and Maid Marian (and as many of his Merry Men as the producers can afford), and eventually the wicked uncle – who is sometimes identified as the Sheriff of Nottingham, Robin's arch-enemy – is made to pay for and/or repent of his crimes.

But loke ye do no husbonde harme, That tilleth with his ploughe. No more ye shall no gode yeman That walketh by grene wode shawe, Ne no knyght ne no squyer That wol be a gode felawe. These bisshoppes and these archebishoppes, Ye shall them bete and bynde; The hye sherif of Notyingham, Hym holde ye in your mynde.

The perfect pantomime hero!

The addition of Robin Hood to the story was probably what saved *Babes in the Wood* as a pantomime. Pantos must end happily and *Babes in the Wood* didn't. It also lacked a hero and heroine, and Robin and Maid Marian were the perfect candidates. Sometimes – rather oddly, I feel – Marian is the Babes' nurse.

The two Babes – always a brother and sister – are normally today played by children, although they have been played by adults in the past. Most memorably at Drury Lane in 1897 they were played by Dan Leno and Herbert Campbell. That must have been quite a production, for although Leno was quite small, Campbell was over six feet tall and weighed 19 stone.

Now *Babes* has fallen from favour. It is difficult to say why. It was regularly produced up until the 1970s – I remember in the mid-1970s working on one production at the Sunderland Empire which had singer Frank Ifield as Robin Hood – but then the number of professional productions began to decline. Qdos Entertainment, the biggest independent pantomime production company in the UK, does not have a single production planned for the 2003–04 season, nor did it produce one in the previous two seasons. In fact, a survey of all the major producers has found only three productions in the last three years – and they were all from the same stable.

The American theatre critic Clive Barnes once memorably said of British musicals that one comes out 'whistling the scenery'. Perhaps *Babes* simply doesn't give enough opportunity for spectacular effects. Cinderella has her transformation scene, Aladdin his magic carpet, Jack has to climb the beanstalk and fight with the giant, Dick Whittington's ship sinks and foliage envelopes Beauty's castle. Perhaps if someone were to come up with an idea that would make us 'whistle the scenery', we might see more of *Babes in the Wood*.

RAY SPENCER

Ray Spencer (left) is director of the Customs House in South Shields, Tyne and Wear. Its pantomime is one of the most successful in the north east. In 2002–03 Mother Goose *ran from 5 December to 11 January and played 60 performances to over 21,000 people – an attendance of 89 per cent. Ray took over direction of the Customs House panto in 1995 and became theatre director in 2000.*

Spencer's first panto was in 1974, as a chorus member of *Sleeping Beauty* for the local amateur group, and he's done at least one panto every year since, directing around 30. His record was the year in which he directed two and appeared in another two. He was, he admits, absolutely shattered at the end of it all.

His first professional panto as director was in 1989: a tour in which they played 61 dates in 23 days, from Dumfries to North Yorkshire.

'We played schools, community centres, youth clubs, working men's clubs – the lot,' he remembers. 'Most days we did three shows – not just in different venues but usually in different towns! If we were playing a school, they'd want us to start around nine in the morning, so that meant leaving around six. We were totally self-contained, so we'd arrive, set up, then get on the make-up and costumes ready to start. We'd do the show, take everything down, pack it into the van and off we'd go to the next, usually starting there about two. Then we'd do it all again in the evening, and, if we were really lucky, we'd get home about ten.'

Not only was it a punishing schedule, but it could get quite dangerous.

'I remember playing a Working Men's Club in Dunfermline,' he says. 'There were 600 kids in the audience. They were given goody bags with all sort of things in them. The parents got the kids settled down – and then left! We got pelted with the contents of the goody bags: Goldilocks was hit by a plastic bottle and I had an orange thrown at me. The cast wanted to call the whole thing off so I had to persuade them to carry on. However, near the end of the show we were rescued. Santa Claus walked in and they mugged him!'

So what is the attraction of panto for him?

'Well, it's tremendous fun – hard work but fun. There's a camaraderie about panto, too. It's a very special time of year and panto is an important part of the magic of Christmas. It's great hearing the audience laugh. And anyway, it also stops you having to go to all those bloody awful Christmas parties!'

In his time, Ray has played Villain, Lead Comic and Dame.

'There are some fabulous acting roles in panto. Villains are great, and Buttons is one of the best parts for any actor. There's so much scope and, of course, you're not restricted by a script. If anything goes wrong in a straight play, you've got to cover up and prevent the audience noticing, but in a panto you do all you can to make the audience aware of it – and get more laughs!'

So there's no sign of him giving up yet, even after almost 30 years?

'Not at all! I just won't be playing Dame again. That's the one part I don't enjoy much: too much faff! I played Ugly Sister a couple of years ago and in one performance I felt there was something wrong but couldn't work out what. "There's nothing wrong," Bob Stott [the other Ugly Sister, right in picture] told me. But all the time we were onstage I knew something wasn't right. In the dressing room at interval I said to him, "Bob, there is something. I just don't know what it is." He simply smiled and pointed to the dressing room door. Hanging on the hook was my bra – I'd just played the most flat-chested Dame ever!

'So, yes, I'll keep on doing panto for as long as I can – but just don't ask me to play Dame!'

THE BUSINESS OF PANTOMIME

Panto keeps theatre alive! That is not an exaggeration. There are many professional theatres – and even more amateur groups – that only survive because of their pantomimes.

Panto season is the one time of the year when even the largest theatres can guarantee houses of 80, 90 or even 100 per cent. Amateur groups will run the panto for longer than any other production they stage, and they'll have matinées on one or even two Saturdays. Professional theatres will have numerous matinées every week of a run, which will last a minimum of three weeks and more usually four or five.

Professional theatres' group-booking organizers go into overdrive for the panto season, targeting social clubs, schools, Scouts, Cubs, Girl Guides, Brownies etc. Every group they can think of, from pre-school playgroups to old folks' homes, and they'll make unbeatable offers. One theatre I know of will pay for a coach (or coaches) to bring groups in. They open in the first week of December to catch the end-of-term primary schools' Christmas celebrations. For three or four afternoons a week there's a constant stream of coaches disgorging their excited passengers (and harassed teachers). It is well worth their while, for many of the children insist on coming back with mums and dads, brothers and sisters, and grandparents. It is not just the knock-on effect of children coming back with their families that builds up the finances: it is the ice creams and sweets, fizzy drinks and popcorn, and the panto merchandise which bring the money rolling in.

Kids' audiences are wonderful for theatres, because they spend, spend, spend – much more than an equivalent-sized adult audience. Profit margins on what the kids buy are far bigger than those on the typical items that adults buy. There's much more profit on a fizzy drink than there is on a pint of beer, and kids consume fizzy drinks by the gallon.

For most theatres, the pantomime is the goose that lays the golden egg, and can make the difference between financial viability and loss (or, regrettably, all too often between acceptable loss and disaster). But it's not just theatres that benefit. There are numerous small-scale theatre companies which keep themselves afloat by touring rather than playing in one theatre. Quite a number of entertainment agencies will stage a touring panto, possibly building it around one of their up-and-coming acts and hiring in actors to fill the rest of the parts.

It is a hard life: meet at eight, or even seven, in the morning; load up the van; drive to the first gig; fit up everything (set, lighting, sound equipment); into make-up and costume; do the gig; remove make-up and costume, then take down set; load the van; off to the afternoon gig; and go through it all again. There's a pretty good chance there will be an evening performance too, so it's all to do again. When you get back to base, the van has to be unloaded. If

Left: The magic of *Peter Pan*, from a 2002–3 production.

Opposite: Russ Abbot as Idle Jack in *Dick Whittington* in 2002.

they're lucky, the performers get home at about ten at night.

As one young actor, Wayne Miller who has played Dame in half a dozen of these touring shows, says: 'By the time you get back to base, you're shattered. Then you have to decide: do you go home to bed, or to the pub? You know you should go to bed, but you're so strung up that you know you won't sleep, so you head off to the pub. With a bit of luck you'll get five or six hours sleep, then you're off again. You start to hope that someone will cancel, so you can kip down in the van for a couple of hours. Towards the end of the run you do just head off to bed as soon as you get back. You're too tired to do anything else.'

All this and often only for the Equity minimum wage (£255 a week in 2003) plus some subsistence expenses.

At the other end of the scale, there are the pantos in theatre venues. At the time of writing, there were 132 professional pantos planned for the 2003–04 season, of which 77 are produced by just eight companies. One company, Qdos Entertainment, is producing 28 – over one fifth of all professional pantomimes in the UK. These pantos, of course, don't tour. They remain in one theatre. So why do theatres 'hire in' a panto? Why not produce one them-selves? That's what always used to happen, even just 25 years ago.

The answer is economies of scale. A company like Qdos is big enough to commission its own scripts, design and build its own sets, make its own costumes, create its own special effects, plot its own lighting, and then reuse them for years (obviously renewing bits that wear out). These companies can also attract the biggest stars, who know that work will come to them year after year. Their directors are panto specialists. They know the genre and their show inside out. They know what works and what doesn't, and they are expert in dealing with the fragile egos of many stars.

Most rehearsals are carried out in London, where the majority of the performers are based, so there are no accommodation and subsistence expenses for the company during the rehearsal period, which would have to be paid if rehearsals took place in the theatre where the show is to be performed. In fact, if you look at those theatres that are producing their own pantos, many have resident companies who are there throughout the year – the Nottingham Playhouse, for example, or the Birmingham Rep.

It has to be said, though, that today's pantos, very popular and big earners though they may be, still do not have the runs which were common in recent history. Today, most professional pantos run from mid-December to mid-January. A five-week run is usual; a run of seven weeks exceptional. When I first worked on a professional panto in the late 1960s, a two-month run was the norm (sometimes even longer) and Saturdays (and occasionally Wednesdays during the school holidays) were three-show days: one in the morning, one in the afternoon and one in the evening. It was a punishing schedule and probably counter-productive. With the best will in the world – and panto performers put everything into what they do – it is impossible to keep the show fresh and full of life when you're doing ten shows a week for two months.

Yet people did it, and they continue to do so, although under slightly less gruelling conditions. Panto is a mad, mad world, but it gets to you. Once it gets its hook into you, you keep coming back for more. Ask anyone who's involved, from the likes of John Inman to the guy down the street who always appears in the local church group's panto, and they'll tell you: there's nothing like it!

LATE NEWS!

Extra! Extra! Read all about it! Goldilocks makes a comeback!
The three bears return to the British stage!

We have looked at a number of pantos in decline; pantos that have fallen from favour and are rarely seen on the professional stage. Now there are signs that one which has been absent from our stages for a number of years is making a comeback. Panto giant Qdos Entertainment's programme is a good indicator of what is popular – they really know the business! – and a look at their programme for 2001 to 2004 suggests that *Goldilocks and the Three Bears* may be making a return to popularity. In 2001–2 they had a production at the Wolverhampton Grand, then in 2002–3 there were two, at the Cliffs Pavilion in Southend and the Swansea Grand. In the 2003–4 season there is yet another production, at Darlington Civic. Another producer also had a production in the 2002–3 season, at Theatre Colwyn in Wales.

Goldilocks was never a major player in the panto stakes, although it did have a number of productions during the Victorian Age. Perhaps its time is coming? You never can tell!

Below: The Three Bears in an amateur panto at the Royalty Theatre, Sunderland.

THE BIG PANTO LIST

Have you ever wondered how many different pantomime titles have been produced over the years? This is an (incomplete) attempt to list them. Variations have been omitted, so *Babes in the Wood*, for example, will also cover *Robin Hood and the Babes in the Wood*, otherwise the list would be as long as the rest of the book! I have also omitted those pantomimes that unite a number of regular stories into one. Where possible I have given dates of the first (and, often, only) production.

All of the pantos in this list have, at one time or another, been produced professionally in a major theatre, either in London or in the provinces. I have not mentioned those that have only been produced by amateurs, nor those that have been devised or produced by small-scale touring companies.

Aladdin and his Wonderful Lamp

Ali Baba and the Forty Thieves

Baa Baa Black Sheep

Babes in the Wood

Bang Up!; or, Harlequin Prime (1810)

Beauty and the Beast

Bluebeard

Broad Grins; or, Harlequin Mag and Harlequin Tag
    (1815 – a parody)

Cinderella

Cock Robin

Conrad and Medora; or, Harlequin Corsair and the
    Little Fairy at the Bottom of the Sea

Davy Jones: or, Harlequin and Mother Carey's
    Chickens (1830)

Dick Whittington

Dido and Aeneas; or, Harlequin, a Butler, a Pimp,
    a Minister of State, Generalissimo, and Lord
    High Admiral, dead and alive again, and at
    last crown'd King of Carthage by Dido (early
    eighteenth century – a parody)

Dr Hocus-Pocus; or, Harlequin Washed White (1814)

The Fair One with the Golden Locks

Fashion's Fools; or, Aquatic Harlequin

The Frog Prince

Furibond; or, Harlequin Negro

Genius of Nonsense

The Golden Goose

Goldilocks and the Three Bears

Goody Two Shoes

The Grand Old Duke of York

Grim Goblin

Grimalkin the Great

Gulliver's Travels

The Hag of the Forest (1829)

Hansel and Gretel

Harlequin and Humpo; or, Columbine by Candlelight

Harlequin Amulet; or, the Magic of Mona

Harlequin Asmodeus; or, Cupid on Crutches (1810)

Harlequin's Chaplet

Harlequin Cock Robin and Jenny Wren; or, Fortunatus and the Water of Life, The Three Bears, The Three Gifts, The Three Wishes, and The Little Man Who Woo'd the Little Maid (1867 – by W. S. Gilbert)

Harlequin Columbus; or, the Old World and the New

Harlequin Everywhere

Harlequin and the Flying Chest; or, Malek and the Princess Shirine (1823)

Harlequin Fortunatus; or, the Wishing Cup (1779)

Harlequin and Fortunio; or, Shing-Moo and Thun-Tun (1815)

Harlequin and Friar Bacon (1820)

Harlequin Genius; or, the Progress of Free Trade, the Spirit of Improvement, and the Great Exhibition of 1851

Harlequin Harper; or, a Jump from Japan (1813)

Harlequin Hoax (1814)

Harlequin Hudibras; or, Old Dame Durden and the Droll Days of the Merry Monarch

Harlequin's Invasion; or, a Christmas Gambol (1759)

Harlequin Jack of All Trades (1825)

Harlequin King Alfred the Great (1846)

Harlequin King Richard III; or, The Magic Arrow and the Battle of Bosworth Field

Harlequin King Ugly Mug and My Lady Lee of Old London Bridge

Harlequin and the Little Thumb (1831)

Harlequin's Magnet; or, the Scandinavian Sorcerer (1805)

Harlequin Munchausen; or, the Fountain of Love (1818)

Harlequin and Number Nip (1827)

Harlequin and Padmanaba (1823)

Harlequin Pat and the Harlequin Bat; or, The Giant's Causeway (1830)

Harlequin and Poor Robin (1823)

Harlequin Quicksilver; or, the Gnome and the Devil (1804)

Harlequin and the Red Dwarf (1812)

Harlequin Skeleton

Harlequin Sorcerer (1717)

Harlequin a Sorcerer; with the Loves of Pluto and Proserpine (1725)

Harlequin and the Steam King; or, Perroule's Wishes and the Fairy Frog

Harlequin and the Swans; or, The Bath of Beauty

Harlequin Teague; or, The Giant's Causeway

Harlequin and the Water Kelpie

Harlequin and the Wild Fiend of California; or, the Demon of the Diggings and the Gnome Queen of the Golden Lake (1849)

Harlequin and the Witch of Ludlow (1809)

Hickory Dickory Dock

Hi-Diddle-Diddle (1861)

Hokee-Pokee the Fiend of the Fungus Forest

Hop o' my Thumb

The House that Jack Built

Humpty Dumpty

Jack and Jill

Jack and the Beanstalk

Jack in the Box

Jack the Giant Killer

Jack the Lad (twentieth century – by David Wood)

The Jealous Doctor (1717)

King Humming Top and the Land of Toys

Lindley Murray's Grammar; or, Harlequin A.E.I.O.U. and Y.

Little Bo-Peep

Little Boy Blue

Little Jack Horner

Little Miss Muffet

Little Red Riding Hood

The Magician; or, Harlequin a Director (1721)

The Mermaid; or, Harlequin Pearl-Diver

Merry Sherwood; or, Harlequin Forrester (1795)

Mother Bunch and the Yellow Dwarf (1821)

Mother Shipton

The Necromancer; or, Harlequin Doctor Faustus (1723)

The Necromancer; or, Harlequin Executed (1723)

Old King Cole

Old Mother Hubbard

The Old Woman of Threadneedle Street (1842)

Old Woman Tossed in a Blanket

Peter Pan

Peter Wilkins; or, Harlequin and the Flying Women of Loadstone Lake

The Pied Piper of Hamelin

Puss in Boots

The Queen Bee; or, Harlequin and the Fairy Hive (1828)

The Queen of Hearts

Queen Mab (1750)

Rapunzel

Rasselas

Red Rufus; or, Harlequin Fact, Fiction and Fancy

Riquet with the Tuft

Robin Hood and his Merry Men

Robinson Crusoe

Romeo and Juliet; or, Harlequin Queen Mab and the World of Dreams

The Royal Chace; or, Merlin's Cave

Rumplestiltskin

Santa Claus

Shakespeare versus Harlequin (1820)

Sinbad the Sailor

Sing a Song of Sixpence

Sleeping Beauty

Snow White and Rose Red

Snow White and the Seven Dwarfs

Spitz-Spitz, the Spider Crab (1875)

The Swans; or, the Beauty of Bath (1813)

The Talisman of Orosmanes; or, Harlequin Made Happy (1794)

Tom the Piper's Son

Tom Thumb

The Touchstone; or, Harlequin Traveller

Tumbledown Dick; or, Phaeton in the Suds (1736 – parody by Henry Fielding)

Twinkle, Twinkle Little Star; or, Harlequin Jack Frost (1970)

Uncle Tom and Lucy Neal; or, Harlequin Liberty and Slavery (1852)

Valentine and Orson; or, Harlequin and the Magic Shield

Walooka and Noomahee; or, the Ape of the Island (1825)

The White Cat

The Witch of the Lakes; or, Harlequin in the Hebrides

The Wonders of Derbyshire; or, Harlequin in the Peak

FURTHER READING

The Encyclopedia of Pantomime
Edited by David Pickering
Gale Research International Ltd (1993)
This has to be the standard work on the subject. It's not a book you sit down and read from cover to cover (although there are a couple of chapters where you can do so), but it's a reference book for all who are interested in panto.

The Pantomime Book
By Paul Harris
Peter Owen Publishers (1996)
A fascinating and entertaining compilation of pantomime jokes, sight-gags and sketches.

Discovering Pantomime
By Gyles Brandreth
Shire Publications (1973)
Now out of print, but worth reading.

Commedia dell'Arte: An Actor's Handbook
By John Rudkin
Routledge (1994)

Commedia dell'Arte: A Handbook for Troupes
By John Rudkin and Olly Crick
Routledge (2001)

It's Behind You – The Magic of Pantomime
www.its-behind-you.com
Nigel Ellacott's website devoted to all things pantomime.
Undoubtedly the best panto site on the Net.

Sur La Lune Fairy Tales
www.surlalunefairytales.com
One of the best reference websites for the origins of many favourite and older but almost forgotten pantos.

INDEX

ACKNOWLEDGEMENTS

My grateful thanks to the following people who have contributed so much to the making of this book: patient editors Jo, Deborah and Jane at New Holland Publishers; Nigel Ellacott, who, with Peter Robbins, forms the Ugly Sisters duo and whose website is an inspiration; Laura Taylor from Qdos for unstinting help with picture research; John Inman for his authoritative insights into panto; Ray Spencer for so many brilliant pantos and being willing to talk about them; Robin Byers at the Customs House for magically producing photographs seconds after being asked; Sarah Clarke at Sunderland Empire for tracking down bits of information I had forgotten, and Roy Todds who, when he was director of the Sunderland Empire, gave a keen but green young theatre photographer (me!) his first chance.

PICTURE CREDITS

Grateful thanks to all the pantomime stars, production companies, photographers and picture libraries who gave permission for the reproduction of the images in this book. Every effort has been made by the publishers to trace the copyright-holders for the images reproduced.

The publishers extend their thanks to the following, who loaned their pictures for inclusion in this book:

Simon Bashford: pages 5, 69 (photograph by W. A. Bennett)

Nigel Ellacott: pages 30, 114, 124, 127, 139 (photograph by Alan Wood)

Rex Features Picture Library: pages 56 (photograph by Rex Features), 60 (photograph by Tony Larkin), 61 (photograph by Peter Brooker), 62 (photograph by Reg Wilson), 72 (photograph by Richard Gardner), 75 (Dezo Hoffmann Collection), 82 (photograph by Rex Features), 84 (Dragon News & Picture Agency), 106–107 (photograph by Tony Larkin), 133 (photograph by Tony Larkin)

Peter Lathan: pages 21, 27, 29, 54, 68, 86, 89, 95, 97, 98, 109, 113, 116, 117, 128 (bottom)

Ian Liston, Hiss & Boo Ltd: pages 40, 42–43, 70, 105, 110

Mander & Michenson Theatre Collection: pages 10, 12, 14, 15 (top), 15 (bottom), 16 (top), 20, 22, 25, 26, 31, 33, 34, 36, 38, 41, 47, 48, 49, 50, 51, 53, 57, 66, 73, 76–77, 80, 82, 87, 90

Mary Evans Picture Library: pages 16 (bottom), 19, 24, 32, 35, 39, 115, 125, 126

Mercers': page 118 (artist: John Glover)

Pictorial Press: pages 13, 23, 58, 59, 63, 74, 85, 100

Qdos Entertainment: pages 9, 44 (photograph by Ralph Hall), 64, 67, 79 (photograph by Stuart Colwill), 88 (photograph by Ralph Hall), 91 (photograph by Stuart Colwill), 93 (photograph by Stuart Colwill), 128, 132, 140

Ray Spencer: page 131

Keith Stitt: page 134

Andrew Ryan: page 71

V&A Images, the Victoria and Albert Museum, London: pages 18 and 103

Paul Welch: page 121